Mediterranean Diet Cookbook

With Over 100 Best Healthy Food Recipes, Meal Plan to Lose Weight

Inna Volia

Contents

Introduction

The temperatures around the Mediterranean Sea are known to produce some delicious dishes that are suitable for the overall good health and well being. A typical Mediterranean diet consist of lots of vegetables, legumes, wholegrain cereals, seeds and nuts with moderate intake of fish and white meat alongside very minimal intake of red meat. The diet also includes consumption of healthy fats and mono-saturated oils such as olive oil which plays such an integral part in the diet. Polyunsaturated fats that are extracted from oily fish, nuts and seeds also form part of Mediterranean diet.

Various studies that have been carried on the diet have proved the numerous benefits that one gets to enjoy when following the diet. Mediterranean diet is packed with flavor filled and delicious foods that are quiet appealing given the colorful combination of the foods. Enhanced use of natural foods and healthy oils such as the olives helps greatly in not only impacting the overall health of the heart and the entire body; the diet is also great with weight loss. Understanding what the diet entails is however vital if one is to maximize the benefits of Mediterranean diet.

Mediterranean Diet Cookbook is a book that's fully packed with in depth information on what Mediterranean diet entails. It has covered detailed understanding of Mediterranean diet, the Mediterranean pyramid which expresses how the diet can be adopted for overall good health. It also covers the numerous benefits associated with Mediterranean diet and a 7 day meal plan that one can work with as a guide especially those who are on the diet for the benefit of weight loss. Mediterranean diet is quite easy to adapt to given the diverse food options that can be consumed while on the diet.

To effectively realize weight loss, one should be willing to engage in more physical exercises and be able to adopt Mediterranean diet as a lifestyle and not just as a diet that can be followed for a short time. Tangible results may be realized after some period of use so commitment to the lifestyle can greatly help towards the realization of the desired benefits. This book is also packed with 100 delicious recipes that you can take advantage of. Regardless of your choice of food, you'll be able to get a recipe that you can easily prepare and that's a fact that makes sustaining the diet much easier.

I encourage you to read the book all through and get to sample some of the recipes that you can start off with. As much as there is a meal plan, you can as well prepare your own meal plan with the given recipes. Ensure that you take the foods in the right portions and give priority to the plant based foods if you're to reap great benefits.

Chapter 1

Understanding Mediterranean Diet

What is Mediterranean diet?

Mediterranean diet is inspired by the diverse and extraordinary countries that surround the Mediterranean Sea such as Greece, Italy, and Spain alongside Middle Eastern and other North African countries. The diet involves consumption of high amounts of unrefined cereals, legumes, olive oils and fish with moderate to high consumption of fish products and vegetables. Dairy products such as yoghurt and cheese should be consumed in moderation as well with very low consumption of meat products. A perfect plate that clearly reflects a Mediterranean diet should be nutritionally balanced. The diet should be quite diverse and full of color, texture and flavor.

Mediterranean diet is mostly crisp and deep with purple grapes, vibrant rainbow carrots with ruby salmon and nutty. The diet should never be restrictive and should instead embrace an enlightened way of consuming plant based foods such as fruits, vegetables, nuts and seeds, healthy grains and legumes. The Mediterranean diet is generally a low fat diet although consumption of healthy mono-saturated fats such as from the olive oils is encouraged. Other healthy polyunsaturated fat from the omega 3 fatty acids which is extracted from certain fish and seafood products is also encouraged. Consumption of unhealthy fats which is mostly found in the processed foods is not encouraged. Consumption of red meat should be limited to very low intake like once or twice within a month.

As much as Mediterranean diet is mostly plant based, it's not an exclusively vegetarian diet. Consumption of foods such as fish, seafood and poultry are encouraged but should be taken in moderation. Foods like whole grains, vegetables, legumes, fruits, nuts and seeds forms the basis of the diet and should be given priority in every meal. The social component and lifestyle when on the diet is another key factor that's worth considering. Eating, sharing meals and having a glass of wine in moderation are other aspects of the Mediterranean diet. Drinking of plenty of water is also encouraged as it improves digestion and overall functioning of the body. Physical activity should also be part of your daily routine when on Mediterranean diet. You can engage in activities such as biking, taking a walk or any other physical activity that you find yourself to be comfortable with.

People are increasingly embracing healthy eating patterns and diets that lead overall body health and lose of weight such as Mediterranean diet should be embraced. Mediterranean diet is one of the diets that are increasingly rising in popularity due to the numerous benefits it's associated with. Since heart disease has been proven to be one of the leading causes of death, embracing a diet that enhances overall health of the heart is quite vital. Conditions such as poor diet, obesity, lack of engaging in physical activity and diabetes are major causes of death and such can be controlled when one is on a healthy diet.

Key Components of Mediterranean Diet
In summary, the Mediterranean focuses on the following;

- Consumption of foods that are plant based such as vegetables, fruits, legumes, nuts and whole grains.
- Consumption of healthy oils such as canola oil and olive oil.
- Use of spices and herbs instead of the processed flavored foods.

- Consumption of red food should be limited to very low or even be discouraged at all.
- Drinking of wine in moderation and plenty of water.
- Engaging in plenty of exercise.
- Having meals with family and friends is a major part of the Mediterranean diet as well.

Grains that are consumed across the Mediterranean region are generally whole grain and have very low levels of unhealthy Tran's fats. Bread is also consumed while on the diet but mostly with a dip of oil and not margarines that has Tran's fats. Nuts are also commonly consumed but should be kept to about a handful a day given their high calorie content.

Mediterranean Pyramid

The Mediterranean diet pyramid was developed to help people all over the world in understanding what the diet entails and how it could be implemented for overall health and well being. The base of the pyramid consists of engaging in activities such as physical exercises and social connections and as you move upwards you'll find some of the core foods that you should put emphasis on. The Mediterranean pyramid should act just as a guideline and not that you consume the actual foods shown on the pyramid. A meal plan acts as a good guideline to help with staying on course if you're to realize the benefits of the diet.

The Mediterranean diet pyramid consists of foods that can be consumed on a daily basis and forms the basis of the diet with those that should be eaten on moderation At the top of the pyramid are those foods that should be consumed once in a while. Remember that embracing the diet entails making simple yet very profound changes in your way of eating each day of your life. It's more like a lifestyle and a way of life. The Mediterranean lifestyle as shown in the pyramid below doesn't just entail prioritizing specific types of foods, it also involves paying much attention to the foods you're selecting for consumption. It also helps in expressing the composition and how you should serve the foods if you're to realize the desired benefits.

The pyramid gives priority to plant based foods that helps in providing the vital nutrients alongside other protective substances that helps in contributing to the overall health and wellbeing of an individual. The foods should be consumed in higher proportions with those in the middle consumed in moderation and those at the top consumed in a restrictive way.

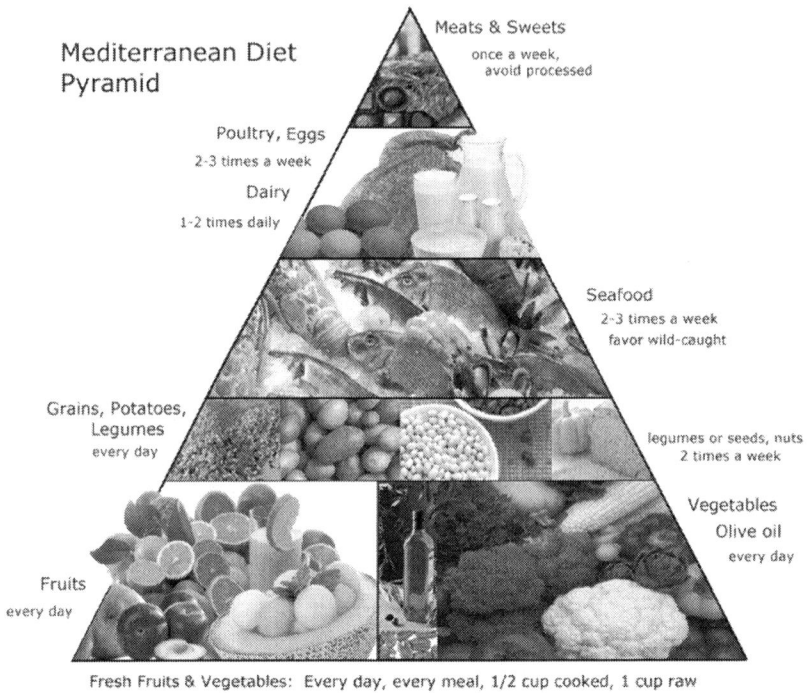

Mediterranean Diet Pyramid

Meats & Sweets
once a week, avoid processed

Poultry, Eggs
2-3 times a week

Dairy
1-2 times daily

Seafood
2-3 times a week
favor wild-caught

Grains, Potatoes, Legumes
every day

legumes or seeds, nuts
2 times a week

Vegetables
Olive oil
every day

Fruits
every day

Fresh Fruits & Vegetables: Every day, every meal, 1/2 cup cooked, 1 cup raw

Foods to focus on

When on Mediterranean diet your focus should be on consuming vegetables, nuts and seeds, legumes, tubers and whole grains. Emphasis should be given to these foods as they form the basis of the diet. Foods such as fish and other seafood, poultry, eggs, dairy, herbs, spices and healthy fats should be taken with moderation. Ensure that you drink plenty of water with moderate levels of red wine, tea and coffee.

Foods to be avoided

There are certain foods that you have to avoid consuming if you're to realize the full benefits of Mediterranean diet. Foods that have added sugar, heavily processed foods, and those containing refined carbohydrates should be avoided if one is to realize the benefits of the diet.

Food like candies, sodas, ice cream often has sugar as one of the ingredients and should be avoided. Pasta and white bread that has been made using refined wheat should also be avoided. Tran's fats such as margarine alongside other processed foods should also be avoided. Refined oils, highly processed foods and processed meat should be avoided.

Chapter 2

Benefits of being on Mediterranean Diet

Mediterranean diet involves consumption of ingredients and foods that are quite close to nature, a fact that makes them ideal for improved health. Being on a Mediterranean diet comes with numerous health benefits and weight loss amongst others. Below are some of the benefits associated with being on Mediterranean diet;

Weight Loss

As much as Mediterranean diet is not focused on weight loss, the healthy way of eating leads to weight loss. Avoiding consumption of processed foods, refined oils and other sugar packed foods results to weight loss. To realize sustained weight loss when on the diet, one needs to incorporate regular exercising just as required when one is on the diet. The fact that Mediterranean diet is low in calories also helps in enhancing weight loss. To realize weight loss when on Mediterranean diet; you should remember that it's not a quick fix and emphasis should be given to overall lifestyle change. Exercising regularly and monitoring the portions that you take should be considered if you're to realize sustained weight loss.

Being on Mediterranean diet works effectively for weight loss because it entails consumption of nutrient dense foods which then enables one to naturally lose weight

Heart Health and disease control

Heart disease has become quite common given the unhealthy way of eating that people tend to follow amongst other challenges. It's however been proven that being on Mediterranean can in a great way help with improving heart health and reducing heart related diseases. Intake of mono-saturated fats, the omega 3 fatty acids from fish and seafood alongside putting focus on vegetables and fruits enhances heart health which then leads to reduced cases of cardiovascular complications and other heart related diseases. Consumption of olive oil has been proven to help with reduction of high blood pressure and also helps in lowering hypertension. Olive oil also helps with combating diseases that arise as a result of oxidation.

Some of the health conditions and diseases that being on Mediterranean can effectively help with include diabetes, cancer, depression and cognitive decline. A diet that consists of higher intake of fresh plant based foods and other healthy fats help with enhancing longevity. Various studies have proven that those suffering from such conditions tend to realize great improvement in their health and recovery from such conditions when on Mediterranean diet. A diet that's low in sugar like Mediterranean diet and includes plenty of fats and fresh produce helps in preventing or even treating diabetes.

Improves cognitive health and mood

Being on Mediterranean diet helps with memory improvement and enhances cognitive health. It's also a great step towards the natural way of treating dementia and Alzheimer's disease. Intake of omega 3 fatty acid amongst other foods that are consumed when on Mediterranean diet has minerals and nutrients that help with enhancing the production of feel good hormones in the brain. Conditions such as stress can in a great way impact one's effectiveness negatively. Eating the traditional foods that are rich in diverse nutrients therefore helps with stress relief. Engaging in physical activity and socialization which is part of Mediterranean diet lifestyle helps with improving one's mood and overall feeling of the body.

Mediterranean Diet Meal Plan to enhance Weight Loss

Having a meal plan can help you stay focused with the diet as you'll know how to balance your meals so as to realized balanced diet that leads to weight loss.

7 Day Mediterranean Meal Plan (1500 calories)

Day 1: Breakfast

Oatmeal, fruits and nuts

- Oatmeal ½ cups cooked with water ½ cup, and skim milk, ½ cup.
- Diced medium apple – ½
- Chopped walnuts – 1 tablespoon
- Honey – 2 tablespoons
- Top the oatmeal with walnuts, honey, apple and a pinch of cinnamon.

Total calories – 327

Snack:

- Apple medium -1
- Peanut butter – 1 tablespoon

Total calories - 200

Lunch:

Spiced chickpea nuts with green salad

- Mixed greens – 2 cups
- Cucumber slices – ½ cup
- Cherry tomatoes – 8 (halved)
- Feta cheese – 1 ½ tablespoons
- Pitted kalamata olives
- Spiced chickpea nuts – ¼ cup
- Combine all the ingredients then with salad, balsamic vinaigrette, olive oil each ½ tablespoon.

Total calories - 373

Snack:

- Boiled egg that's seasoned with salt and pepper -1

Calories – 78

Dinner:

- Roast salmon with couscous and fennel
- Roasted salmon fillet – 5 oz
- Coated with dried oregano, ¼ teaspoon, olive oil ¼ teaspoon, salt and pepper for seasoning.
- Roasted fennel bulb – 1 cup tossed with salt and pepper, olive oil ½ tablespoons.
- Whole wheat couscous – 1 cup topped with chopped walnuts – 1 ½ tablespoon
- Garnish with lemon wedge.

Calories – 480

- Snack: Medium fresh fig – 1

Calories – 37

MEDITERRANEAN DIET COOKBOOK

Day 2: Breakfast

Oatmeal, fruits and nuts

- Cooked oatmeal ½ cup with water ½ cup and skim milk ½ cup
- Sliced strawberries – ½ cup
- Chopped walnuts – 1 tablespoons
- Honey – 2 teaspoons
- Top the oatmeal with a pinch of cinnamon, honey and walnuts.

Calories - 319

Snack:

- 2 clementines

Calories - 70

Lunch

Spiced chickpea nuts with green salad

- Mixed greens – 2 cups
- Cucumber slices – ½ cup
- Cherry tomatoes – 8 (halved)
- Feta cheese – 1 ½ tablespoon
- Top with spiced chickpea nuts – 1 serving
- Pitted kalamata olives – 8
- Combine all the ingredients then top with olive oil ½ tablespoon and balsamic vinegar.

Calories – 373

Snack:

Walnuts – 5

Dried apricots –

Calories - 108

Dinner:

- Artichoke Gnocchi and tomato 1 ¾ cup
- Mixed greens – 2 cups
- Top with olive oil and balsamic vinegar

Calories – 492

Snack:

Dark chocolate – 1 ounce

Calories – 156

Day 3: Breakfast

Egg and Toast

- Toasted whole wheat bread - 1 slice
- Mashed avocado – ½
- An egg cooked with olive oil and seasoned with salt and pepper
- Top the toast with an egg and avocado.
- Clementine – 1

Calories - 347

Snack:

Spiced chickpea nuts – ¼ cups

Calories – 131

Lunch

Left overs:

Artichoke Gnocchi and tomato that's topped with feta cheese 1 tablespoon

Mixed greens – 2 cups

Grated carrot – 2 tablespoons

Top the salad with olive oil and balsamic vinaigrette each ½ tablespoon

Snack:

Walnuts – 8

Medium apple: 1

Dinner:

- Cooked cod seasoned with preferred herbs and olive oil – 1 teaspoon
- Cherry tomatoes – ½ cup, sautéed sliced zucchini 1cup, olive oil, ½ tablespoon and seasoned with pepper and salt.
- Whole wheat couscous (cooked) – 1 cup
- Toasted whole wheat pita - ½
- Garnish with lemon

Calories - 447

Day 4: Breakfast

Whole wheat toast – 1 slice

Peanut butter – 1 ½ tablespoon

Medium banana – 1

Calories – 331

Snack:

- Halves walnuts – 6

Calories - 78

Lunch

- Pita bread and hummus with green salad
- Mixed greens – 2 cups
- Sliced cucumber – ½ cup
- Grated carrot – 2 tablespoon
- Top salad with balsamic vinegar and olive oil
- Serve with toasted whole wheat pita 1 with hummus ¼ cup for dipping.

Calories – 376

Snack

- Plain Greek yoghurt, ½ that's topped with sliced strawberries ¼ cup

Calories – 80

Dinner

- Egg drop soup (Italian) – 2 cups
- Aragula 2 cups, topped with balsamic vinegar and olive oil – ½ tablespoon
- Whole wheat bread sliced that's toasted and drizzled with olive oil, 1 teaspoon.

Snack

Dark chocolate – 1 oz

Day 5: Breakfast

Oatmeal, fruits and nuts

- Oatmeal ½ cups cooked with water ½ cup, and skim milk, ½ cup.
- Diced medium apple – ½
- Chopped walnuts – 1 tablespoon
- Honey – 2 tablespoons
- Top the oatmeal with walnuts, honey, apple and a pinch of cinnamon.

Total calories – 327

Snack:

- Apple medium -1
- Peanut butter – 1 tablespoon

Total calories - 200

Lunch

- Leftovers
- Egg drop soup (Italian) – 1 ½ cups
- Toasted whole wheat bread – 1 slice
- Aragula, 2 cups topped with balsamic vinegar and olive oil, ½ tablespoon.

Snack:

- Sliced strawberries – 1 cup
- Walnuts –8
- Calories – 151

Dinner

- Roast pork with asparagus and cherry tomato bowl – 1 serving

Calories - 437

Day 6: Breakfast

- Whole wheat toast – 1 slice
- Peanut butter – 1 ½ tablespoon
- Medium banana – 1

Calories – 331

Snack:

Hard boiled eggs, 1 that's seasoned with salt and pepper

Lunch

- Pita bread and hummus with green salad
- Mixed greens – 2 cups
- Sliced cucumber – ½ cup
- Halved cherry tomatoes – 5 (halved)
- Feta cheese – 1 tablespoon
- Combine the ingredients then top the salad with balsamic vinegar and olive oil
- Serve with toasted whole wheat pita 1 with hummus 3 tablespoons for dipping.

Calories – 384

Snack:

Medium apple – 1

Walnut halves – 5

Calories – 160

Dinner

- Mediterranean tuna with spinach salad- 1 serving
- Whole wheat bread that's toasted and drizzled with olive oil 1 teaspoon.

Calories – 486

Snack:

Medium fresh fig – 1

Medium plum – 1

Day 7: Breakfast

Egg and Toast

- Toasted whole wheat bread - 1 slice
- Mashed avocado – ½
- An egg cooked with olive oil and seasoned with salt and pepper
- Top the toast with an egg and avocado.
- Clementine – 1

Calories - 347

Lunch

- Pita bread and hummus with green salad
- Mixed greens – 2 cups
- Sliced cucumber – ½ cup
- Grated carrot – 2 tablespoon
- Top salad with balsamic vinegar and olive oil
- Serve with toasted whole wheat pita 1 with hummus ¼ cup for dipping.

Calories – 376

Snack:

Sliced strawberries – 1 cup

Halves walnuts – 8

Calories – 151

Dinner

- Chicken saltimbocca – 1 serving
- Whole-wheat couscous (cooked) – ¾ cup
- Steamed broccoli florets

Chapter 3

100 Best Food Recipes

Breakfast Recipes

1. Mediterranean Scrambled eggs with Spinach

Preparation and cooking time – 10 minutes

Serves – 2

Ingredients

- Vegetable oil – 1 tablespoon
- Diced and seeded tomato - 1/3 cup
- Baby spinach – 1
- Cubed feta cheese – 2
- Eggs - 3
- Salt and pepper to taste

Instructions

- Place a frying pan over medium heat then add cooking oil
- Sauté the spinach alongside the tomatoes until the spinach gets wilted.
- Add eggs then mix to scramble. Allow to stay for about 30 seconds then add feta cheese
- Cook the mixture until the eggs are well cooked as per your preference.
- Add salt and pepper to season.

Nutritional value

Calories	76.7
Fat	0.7g
Carbohydrate	15.3g
Fiber	5.8g
Protein	6.5g

2. Greek Quinoa Breakfast Bowl

Preparation and cooking time – 30 minutes

Serves – 4

Ingredients

- Eggs – 12
- Plain Greek yoghurt – ¼ cup
- Baby spinach – 1 (5 ounce)
- Halved cherry tomatoes – 1 pint
- Granulated garlic – 1 teaspoon
- Onion powder – 1 teaspoon
- Feta Cheese – 1 cup
- Cooked quinoa – 2 cups
- Olive oil – 1 teaspoon

Instructions

- In a bowl mix together eggs, granulated garlic, Greek yoghurt, onion powder, salt and pepper then set aside.
- Heat olive oil in a large skillet then add spinach and cook until slightly wilted for about 4 minutes.
- Add in the cherry tomatoes then cook until the tomatoes soften for about 4 minutes.
- Stir in the egg mixture then cook until the eggs are ready or for about 7 minutes. Remember to stir the eggs as they cook so as to turn out as scrambled.
- Stir in quinoa and feta once the eggs are scrambled
- Serve hot and enjoy

Nutritional value

Calories	357
Fat	8g
Carbohydrate	20g
Fiber	3g
Protein	23g

3. Banana Nut Oatmeal

Preparation and cooking time – 8 minutes

Serves – 2

Ingredients

- Quick cooking oats – ¼ cup
- Flax seeds – 1 teaspoon
- Skim milk – ½ cup
- Chopped walnuts – 2 tablespoons
- Honey – 3 tablespoons
- Peeled banana – 1

Instructions

- Combine the flax seeds, oats, milk, walnuts, banana and honey in a bowl that's microwave safe.
- Cook the mixture in the microwave for about 3 minutes.
- Mash the banana using a fork then stir into the bowl.
- Serve hot and enjoy

Nutritional value

Calories	240
Fat	1. 5g
Carbohydrate	40g
Fiber	4g
Protein	10g

4. Greek yoghurt, with pomegranate, honey and cinnamon

Preparation and cooking time – 10 minutes

Serves – 1

Ingredients

- Plain Greek yoghurt – ½ cup (Non fat)
- Pomegranate seeds – 1/8 cup
- Honey – for drizzling
- Cinnamon – dash

Instructions

- Place yoghurt into a serving bowl then add pomegranate seeds.
- Drizzle the mixture with honey then sprinkle with cinnamon.
- Stir the mixture and enjoy

Nutritional value

Calories	140
Fat	4g
Carbohydrate	23g
Fiber	1g
Protein	4g

5. Mediterranean Breakfast Burrito

Preparation and cooking time – 25 minutes

Serves – 3

Ingredients

- Tortillas – 6
- Sun dried tomatoes – 10 inches
- Eggs – 9
- Baby spinach – 2 cups
- Black olives – 3 tablespoons
- Feta Cheese – ½ cup (Low fat)
- Refried beans – ¾ cup (canned)
- Dried tomatoes – 3 tablespoons

Instructions

- Use nonstick spray on a medium frying pan then scramble the eggs and toss until the eggs harden.
- Add black olives, spinach, and the sun dried tomatoes and continue to stir until the mixture becomes dry.
- Add feta cheese then cover until the cheese melts

- Add refried beans 2 tablespoons to each of the tortilla then top with the egg mixture as you divide equally between all the burritos then wrap accordingly.
- Grill in a frying pan until well cooked or lightly browned.
- You can serve it hot with your preferred fruit.

Nutritional value

Calories	252
Fat	11g
Carbohydrate	21g
Fiber	2g
Protein	14g

6.   Mediterranean Breakfast Pitas

Preparation and cooking time – 25 minutes

Serves – 3

Ingredients

- Large eggs – 4
- Whole wheat pita – 2
- Hummus- ½ cup
- Medium tomatoes – 2
- Cucumber – 1
- Freshly ground black pepper
- Fresh parsley leaves 1 handful (coarsely chopped)
- Salt to taste

Instructions

- Fill a saucepan with water then bring to boil.
- Place eggs into the water then cook for about 7 minutes. Drain the water then run the eggs in cold water in order to cool.
- Peal the eggs then cut into slices. Sprinkle with salt then set aside.
- Spread with hummus the pita pocket then add cucumber slices and diced tomato into each of the pitas.
- Sprinkle with pepper and salt then tuck a sliced egg into each and sprinkle with hot sauce and parsley.
- Serve and enjoy

Nutritional value

Calories	230
Fat	9g
Carbohydrate	27g
Fiber	6g
Protein	14g

7. Mediterranean halloumi and egg toast

Preparation and cooking time – 25 minutes

Serves – 2

Ingredients

- Pesto – 1 tablespoon
- Olive oil – 3 tablespoon
- Cherry tomatoes – ½ cup
- Eggs - 2
- Cremini mushrooms – 5
- Whole grain artisan bread – 4 slices
- Baby arugula – 1 cup
- Avocado – ½
- Halloumi cheese – 100grams

Instructions

- Into a small bowl combine pesto with olive oil 1 ½ tablespoon
- In another bowl mix cherry tomatoes with the remaining olive oil then set aside.
- In a frying pan add the ½ tablespoon olive oil then add the sliced mushrooms then cooking until browned on the side then add pepper and salt as you stir.
- Allow it to cook over medium heat as you stir until done. Remove then set aside in a plate.
- Use the same pan to fry sliced halloumi cheese until it turns golden on the sides then set aside in a plate.
- Heat ½ tablespoon olive oil with pesto mixture then top each of the plates with aragula, half of mushrooms, half of tomatoes, half of avocado and half of halloumi with one fried egg.
- Season with pepper then serve warm and enjoy

Nutritional value

Calories	500
Fat	14g
Carbohydrate	10g
Fiber	5g
Protein	22g

8. Mediterranean Frittata

Preparation and cooking time – 40 minutes

Serves – 6

Ingredients

- Eggs - 12
- Crumbled goat cheese – 6 ounces
- Roasted red peppers – 1 jar
- Sliced cremini mushrooms – 4 ounces
- Deli ham diced – ¼ pound
- Parmesan cheese freshly grated – ¼ cup
- Olive oil
- Salt

Instructions

- Get the oven preheated to 350°F then in a bowl combine roasted red peppers, eggs, parmesan, goat cheese and salt then whisk all together.
- Coat a cast iron skillet with olive oil then place the pan over medium heat and add the mushrooms.

- Cook for a minute or until soft then add diced ham and fry for one more minute.
- Pour in the egg mixture as you ensure that everything is mixed well and even.
- Transfer to the oven and bake for about 30 minutes or until puffy and golden
- Remove from the oven once ready then let it stay for a few minutes.
- Cut into wedges then serve and enjoy.

Nutritional value

Calories	530
Fat	40g
Carbohydrate	5g
Fiber	1g
Protein	41g

9. Roasted red pepper olive with mozzarella on toast

Preparation and cooking time – 30 minutes

Serves – 6

Ingredients

- Pitted kalamata leaves – ½ cup
- Lemon juice – 1 tablespoon
- Olive oil – ¼ cup
- Capers – 1 tablespoon
- Aleppo pepper – ½ teaspoon
- Ground cumin – 1 teaspoon
- Onion powder – ½ teaspoon
- Garlic powder – ½ teaspoon
- Cardamom – ¼ teaspoon
- Onion powder – ½ teaspoon
- Chopped cilantro – 2 tablespoon
- Roasted red peppers – 1 cup
- Toasted sourdough bread – 6 pieces
- Thinly sliced fresh mozzarella – 1 lb

Instructions

- Place all the ingredients apart from red peppers, cilantro into a food processor then process until the ingredients are finely chopped.
- Add the roasted red peppers and cilantro into the food processor then process until finely chopped.
- In a bowl, add olive oil and roasted red pepper then mix.
- Cut the roasted slices of bread into half then layer each toast with sliced mozzarella.
- Add some dollop tapenade then serve and enjoy

Nutritional value

Calories	532
Fat	22g
Carbohydrate	30g
Fiber	5g
Protein	20g

10. Mediterranean Breakfast Egg Muffins

Preparation and cooking time – 40 minutes

Serves – 2

Ingredients

- Cooking oil spray
- Skimmed milk – 2 tablespoons
- Large eggs – 2
- Finely chopped leek – 35g
- Grated parmesan cheese – 4 tablespoons
- Chopped tomato with seeds removed – 1
- Finely chopped spinach – 25g
- Freshly ground pepper
- Salt
- Grated cheddar cheese – 25g

Instructions

- Get the oven preheated to 350°F
- Spray muffin tin with the cooking spray then in a pouring jug whisk eggs, parmesan cheese and milk together and season.
- Pour the mixture into each of the muffin cup then mix with chopped vegetables.
- Divide grated cheddar cheese then top the muffin cups.
- Place into the oven then bake for about 20 minutes or until the egg gets set.

Nutritional value

Calories	308
Fat	9.7g
Carbohydrate	8.7g
Fiber	1.7g
Protein	24.4g

11. Mediterranean Omellete

Preparation and cooking time – 15 minutes

Serves – 1

Ingredients

Olive oil or butter – 1 teaspoon

Eggs – 2

Milk – 1 tablespoon

Oregano

Salt and pepper

Sliced kalamata – 2 tablespoons

Diced tomato - 2 tablespoons

Feta cheese – 1 tablespoon

Artichoke hearts – 1

Romesco sauce – 1 tablespoon

Instructions

- In skillet heat oil then pour the mixture of milk, egg, oregano, salt and pepper into the skillet as you cover the bottom of the pan with it.
- Cook until the eggs sets then sprinkle olive artichoke, tomato and feta to half of the egg then fold over and cover.
- Cook the eggs for a minute or until set then remove from the heat and top with romesco sauce
- Enjoy

Nutritional value

Calories	303
Fat	17.1g
Carbohydrate	21.9g
Fiber	9.9g
Protein	18.2g

12. Sprouted Cinnamon – Maple French Toast

Preparation and cooking time – 8 minutes

Serves – 2

Ingredients

- Eggs – 2
- Ground Cinnamon – 1 teaspoon
- Vanilla extract – 1 teaspoon
- Unsalted butter – 1 tablespoon
- Maple syrup

Instructions

- In a bowl whisk together the eggs, cinnamon, almond milk and vanilla then soak the slices of bread into the egg mixture then allow to stay for about 2 minutes.
- Add butter to a skillet over medium heat then add the bread as you allow to cook for about 2 minutes on both sides or until golden brown.
- Serve toast with a sprinkle of cinnamon and maple syrup.

Nutritional value

Calories	265
Fat	11.1g
Carbohydrate	34.4g
Fiber	2.9g
Protein	8.6g

13. Whole wheat olive and feta cheese bread

Preparation and cooking time – 1hr 45 minutes

Yields– 1 loaf

Ingredients

- Whole wheat flour – 2 cups (250g)
- All purpose flour – 2 cups (250g)
- Instant dry yeast – 2 tablespoons
- Oregano – 3 tablespoons
- Salt – 1 tablespoons
- Chopped olives – 1 ½ cup
- Cup olive oil – ¼ cup
- Crumbled feta cheese – ½ cup
- Lukewarm water – 1 cup

Instructions

- Mix instant yeast and flour into a bowl then add water and mix. Add olive oil, salt and mix well.
- Remove the dough from the bowl then knead as you stretch it and roll it back. Stretch and roll severally until the dough becomes elastic and smooth then roll into a ball as you cover using a plastic wrap then let it stay in a warm place for about 1 hour.
- Take the dough and separate into two balls then stretch it into a long piece of dough. Add the half of the olives, feta, and oregano then form into ball again as you ensures that the olives are inside.
- Flatten the dough on a pan then let it stay for 30 minutes. Get the oven preheated to 425°F then sprinkle flour on each piece as you make a small slit.
- Allow to bake for 30 minutes. The bread may be moist as a result of the feta and the olives.
- Bake the bread in the oven then allow to cool before serving.

Nutritional value

Calories	234
Fat	10.4g
Carbohydrate	29.4g
Fiber	4.4g
Protein	8.4g

14.Pineapple upside down pancakes

Preparation and cooking time – 50 minutes

Serves– 6

Ingredients

- All purpose flour – 1 1/3 cups
- Baking powder – 1 ¼ teaspoons
- Light brown sugar – ½ cup
- Refrigerated coconut milk - 1 cup
- Eggs – 2
- Melted butter – 4 tablespoons
- Ground cinnamon – ¼ teaspoon
- Sliced pineapple – 1
- Extra butter for the griddle

Instructions

- Whisk together in a bowl, baking powder and brown sugar ¼ cup then mixed well. Whisk in the eggs, melted butter, buttermilk, cinnamon and vanilla extract then mix until the butter comes together.

- Over medium heat place a nonstick skillet then melt the remaining butter. Add pineapple ring at the centre of the skillet then sprinkle the remaining brown sugar then turn once it browns.
- Add a cherry over the pineapple ring then pour butter ¼ cup over the pineapple as you allow it to flow outside the ring. Cook until the bubbles form and the bottom gets more sturdy, crisp and golden brown.
- Flip the pancake over entirely with the cherry and the pineapple then cook until it gets crisp and golden brown.
- Remove the pancake then place into a warm oven at a temperature of 225°F.
- Repeat the processes with all the pancakes then serve and enjoy.

Nutritional value

Calories	367
Fat	13.9g
Carbohydrate	58.1g
Fiber	0.9g
Protein	4g

15. Bananas foster French toast

Preparation and cooking time – 40 minutes
Serves– 6slices
Ingredients
French toast:

- Bread of choice – 6 slices
- Eggs – 2
- Vanilla extract – 1 teaspoon
- Granulated sugar – 3 tablespoons
- Ground cinnamon – ½ teaspoon
- Butter
- Pinch of salt

Banana caramel syrup

- Butter – ¼ cup
- Lightly packed brown sugar - ¾ cup
- Whipping heavy cream – 3 tablespoons
- Ground cinnamon – ¼ cup
- Dark rum (Optional) – 4 tablespoons
- Vanilla extract – 1 teaspoon

Instructions

For the French toast:

- Whisk together eggs, cinnamon, vanilla, milk, sugar and salt then set aside. Place a frying pan over medium heat then add a little butter and allow to melt.
- Drip the slices of the bread one at a time into the egg mixture until completely soaked in the liquid.
- Flip the bread over as you repeat with the other side. Add the bread into the frying pan then fry for about 3 minutes on each side until it turns golden brown.

Banana caramel syrup:

- Place a frying pan over medium heat then melt butter then add brown sugar as you gently whisk and combine gently. Let the mixture settle as you boil for two more minutes.
- Add whipping cream as you whisk to combine. Stir the cinnamon and the vanilla then add banana slices and rum.
- Allow to cook for about 1 minutes or you can wait until the bananas becomes soft
- Spoon the caramel syrup and the bananas over French toast then serve immediately and enjoy.

Nutritional value

Calories	495
Fat	15g
Carbohydrate	82g
Fiber	4g
Protein	10g

16.Creamy oatmeal bowls with raspberries, seeds and honey

Preparation and cooking time – 20 minutes

Serves– 3

Ingredients

- Rolled oats – 1 cup
- Boiling water – 2 cups
- Butter – 2 teaspoons
- Ground cinnamon – ½ teaspoon

For the toppings

- Fresh berries or your preferred fruit
- Seeds or nuts of your choice
- Honey to taste

Instructions

- Combine the oats, salt and water into a saucepan then let it boil and cook for about 5 minutes.
- Reduce the heat as you let it simmer for about 10 minutes as you stir regularly or until the oats become creamy with the water absorbed.
- Remove the pan out of heat then add cinnamon and butter as you cover with the lid.
- Let it steam for about 5 minutes then stir the oats again and serve was you top with the nuts, berries and seeds then add a drizzle of honey.

Nutritional value

Calories	324
Fat	10.2g
Carbohydrate	47.9g
Fiber	8.4g
Protein	16.4g

17. Mediterranean veggie dip

Preparation and cooking time – 15 minutes

Serves– 12

Ingredients

- Yoghurt cheese – 1
- Chopped and roasted red sweet pepper – ¼ cup
- Crumbled feta cheese – ¼
- Sliced green onion – 2 tablespoons – 2
- Chopped pitted kalamata – 2
- Fresh Italian parsley – 2 tablespoons
- Low fat plain yoghurt – 1

Dippers: Whole grain crackers, toasted pita bread, broccoli florets, sweet pepper strips or carrot sticks.

Ingredients

- Combine in a bowl the yoghurt cheese, feta cheese, green onion, olives parsley, sweet pepper, oregano, olives and parsley then cover and chill for about 24 hours.
- Stir it before serving then serve with dippers.
- Spoon in the yogurt then refrigerate overnight.

Nutritional value

Calories	33
Fat	1g
Carbohydrate	3g
Fiber	3g
Protein	3g

18.Breakfast skillet hash

Preparation and cooking time – 20 minutes

Serves– 4

Ingredients

- Vegetable Oil – 1 tablespoon – 1
- Hash brown – 4 ½ cups
- Bacon – 1 tablespoon
- Eggs – 4
- Shredded cheddar cheese – ½ cup
- Sliced green onions – 2 tablespoons

Directions

- Place a large nonstick skillet pan over medium heat then add hash browns and all the seasonings. Cook the mixture as you stir until lightly browned or for about 8 minutes.
- Make into 4 indentations as you use a wooden spoon's back then break the eggs into each of the indentation. Sprinkle it with cheese and the green onions as you cover for about 5 minutes or until the eggs are well set.

Nutritional value

Calories	640
Fat	37g
Carbohydrate	62g
Fiber	5g
Protein	16g

19. Breakfast bowl ideas

Preparation and cooking time – 20 minutes

Serves– 4

Ingredients

- Dairy free yoghurt -1 container
- Cooked quinoa – ¼ cup
- Blueberries – ¼ cup
- Pomegranate seeds – 3 tablespoons
- Sliced almonds – 1 tablespoon
- Sliced kiwi – ¼ cup

Instructions

- Mix all the ingredients as you desire then enjoy

20.   Pan fried breakfast potatoes

Preparation and cooking time – 30 minutes

Serves– 2

Ingredients

- Baking potatoes – 2 tablespoons
- Canola oil – 2 tablespoons
- Pinch salt – 1
- Parmesan cheese – ½ tablespoon

Instructions

- Place a medium skillet over medium heat then add canola oil. Add chopped potatoes into the skillet then fry until the potatoes begin t brown on all sides.
- Allow all the sides to brown as the potatoes may take cook differently.

- Transfer the potatoes with a slotted spoon onto a plate that's lined with paper towel.
- Sprinkle the potatoes with parsley, salt and cheese then enjoy.

Nutritional value

Calories	230
Fat	14g
Carbohydrate	21g
Fiber	5g
Protein	6g

21. Breakfast Tacos

Preparation and cooking time – 30 minutes

Serves– 4

Ingredients

- Bacon slices – 6 slices
- Medium diced onions – ¼
- Scrambled eggs – 6
- Corn tortillas – 6
- Pico de gallo to be used for topping

Instructions

- Have the bacon chopped into pieces then add to a pan alongside the diced onion.
- Sauté until well cooked then remove from the pan and drain from grease.
- Scoop the egg mixture the place on the taco shell as you top with the fresh pico de gallo.

22.   Easy breakfast Eggrolls

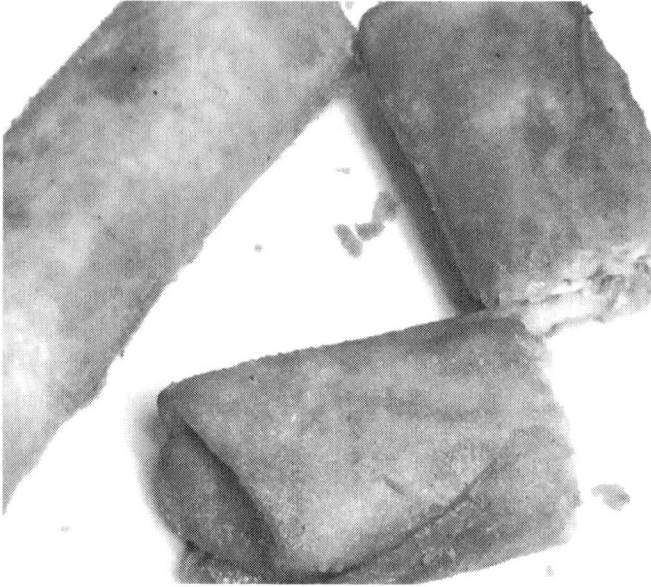

Preparation and cooking time – 25minutes

Serves– 4

Ingredients

- Pastries rolls – 9
- Breakfast sausages – ½ pound
- Chorizo
- Eggs – 6
- Cheddar cheese
- Frying oil

Instructions

- Cook sausage in a skillet until brown then add eggs and stir until scrambled with the sausage.
- Add cheese to the mixture then roll the pastries and let them stay for about two hours before use.

- Add the mixture to the pastry then fold the mixture with the pastry.
- Place sufficient oil into the pan then cover up to half of the egg rolls.
- Once the oil is hot, place the egg roll for 30 seconds on all the sides until browned.
- Serve and enjoy

Nutritional value

Calories	400
Fat	18g
Carbohydrate	44g
Fiber	7g
Protein	19g

23.   Yoghurt and Cashew Breakfast Parfaits

Preparation and cooking time – 10 minutes

Serves– 1

Ingredients

- Greek yoghurt low fat – 5.3 ounce
- Dark chocolate bar and simple roasted cashew – 1.41 ounce
- Coarsely chopped unsalted and toasted cashews – 1 tablespoon
- Sliced strawberries
- Blueberries

Instructions

- Place yoghurt at the bottom of the glass then perfectly add the bar pieces and top with cashews and the berries.
- Serve and joy

24.   **Breakfast Bagel**

Preparation and cooking time – 25 minutes

Serves– 4

Ingredients

- Whole bagels – 2
- Eggs – 2
- Bacon – 1 ounce
- Cheese – 1 ounce
- Haas acocados – 1
- Ground cumin – 1/8 teaspoon
- Chopped cilantro – 1 teaspoon
- Ground cayenne pepper – 1/8 teaspoon
- Salt – 1 teaspoon
- Ketchup – 2 tablespoon
- Sriracha sauce – 1 teaspoon

Instructions

- Cook the bacon and as it cooks, mix in cilantro, avocado and seasonings for the guacamole. Add ketchup 2 tablespoons to sriracha and when the bacon is halfway done, cook the eggs then cover as you toast the bagel.
- Cook for a minute then top the eggs with cheese then cover.
- Once the bacon is ready, set it aside then allow it to cool.
- Once the eggs are cooked split into two then top the bagel with sriracha, then ketchup and the egg. Add the bacon then top with avocado as you add the top bagel.
- Serve and enjoy

Nutritional value

Calories	391
Fat	15g
Carbohydrate	38g
Fiber	2g
Protein	26g

25.   Greek Yoghurt

Preparation and cooking time – 30 minutes

Serves– 5

Ingredients

- Egg – 1
- Sugar – 2 tablespoons
- Baking powder – 1 ½ teaspoon
- Greek yoghurt – 5 tablespoon
- Flour – 6 tablespoons
- Pinch of salt
- Figs cut into quarters
- Honey spread on the slices

Instructions

- Get the oven preheated to 356ºF
- In a bowl, mix eggs, flour, sugar, lemon zest, baking powder and yoghurt.
- Spray the baking dish with some oil then add the mixture into the dish as you add fig quarters on top.
- Allow to bake for 23 minutes
- Serve and enjoy

Nutritional value

Calories	90
Fat	1.5g
Carbohydrate	38g
Fiber	1g
Protein	3g

26.   Moist lemon cake

Preparation and cooking time – 1 hr 5 minutes

Serves – 4

Ingredients

- Yellow cake mix – 1 package
- Vegetable oil – 1 cup
- Lemon pudding – 1 package
- Eggs – 3
- Sugar – 1 ½ cup
- Butter – 2 tablespoons
- Lemon juice – 1/3 cup

Instructions

Get the oven preheated to 350°Fthen add butter to the cake pan then mix together the yellow cake mix with juice, oil and instant puddling. Add the eggs as you beat one at a time then mix until well combined.

Place into the oven then bake for about 50 minutes. Once ready, allow to cool for about 3 minutes then start the glaze.

For the glaze, mix melted butter with sugar and lemon juice then make holes at the top of the cake to the bottom. Pour the glaze over the cake.

Nutritional value

Calories	168
Fat	1g
Carbohydrate	23g
Fiber	0g
Protein	2.1g

27. Chocolate chip cookies

Preparation and cooking time – 30 minutes

Serves – 4

Ingredients

- Sugar – ½ cup
- Brown sugar – ½ cup
- Butter – 1 1/3
- Vanilla – 1 teaspoon
- Eggs – 1
- Baking soda – ½ teaspoon
- Flour 1 ¾ cups
- Semi sweet chocolate morsels - 1 cup
- Salt – ½ teaspoon

Instructions

- Get the oven preheated to 350°F then mix together the first 5 ingredients in a bowl.
- In another bowl mix the dry ingredients as you add then one after another to the creamed mixture.
- Add chocolate then mix and roll into balls on the greased parchment. Bake for about 12 minutes then allow to cool and enjoy.

Nutritional value

Calories	860
Fat	45g
Carbohydrate	111g
Fiber	4g
Protein	9g

MEDITERRANEAN DIET COOKBOOK

Chapter 4

Lunch Recipes

1. Mediterranean Chicken Quinoa bowl

Preparation and cooking time – 30 minutes

Serves– 5

Ingredients

- Trimmed boneless and skinless chicken breasts – 1 pound
- Ground pepper – ¼ teaspoon
- Slivered almonds – ¼ cup
- Extra virgin oil – 4 tablespoons
- Crushed clove garlic – 1
- Ground Pepper – ¼ teaspoon
- Paprika – 1 teaspoon

- Crushed red pepper- ¼ teaspoon
- Cooked quinoa – 2 cups
- Finely chopped kalamata olives
- Diced Cucumber – 1 cup
- Finely chopped fresh parsley – 2 tablespoons
- Crumbled feta cheese – ¼ cup

Instructions

- Have the oven preheated to high then line the baking sheet with foil
- Season the chicken with salt and pepper then place on the baking sheet. Broil it as you turn once for about 18 minutes or until the thermometer inserted in the thick areas reads 165°F. You can then transfer the chicken to a cutting board then shred or slice.
- Place peppers, garlic, cumin, almonds and oil 2 tablespoons into the food processor then process until smooth.
- Combine the olives, quinoa, and the remaining oil into a medium bowl
- To serve, divide quinoa mixture into 4 bowls then top with chicken, cucumber and red pepper sauce. Sprinkle with parsley and feta then enjoy.

Nutritional value

Calories	520
Fat	27g
Carbohydrate	31g
Fiber	4g
Protein	34g

2. Tuscan style tuna salad

Preparation and cooking time – 20 minutes

Serves– 2

Ingredients

- Drained chunk light tuna – 2 cans
- Trimmed and sliced scallions – 4
- Virgin olive oil – 2 tablespoons
- Lemon juice – 2 table spoons
- Salt – ¼ teaspoon
- Quartered cherry tomatoes - 10
- Can of small white beans – 1 15 ounce
- Freshly ground pepper

Instructions

- Combine beans, tomatoes, tuna, scallions, lemon juice, salt and pepper into a bowl then stir gently and refrigerate.
- Remove from the refrigerator then serve and enjoy.

Nutritional value

Calories	199
Fat	9g
Carbohydrate	20g
Fiber	6g
Protein	16g

3. Caprese style portobellos

Preparation and cooking time – 20 minutes

Serves– 3

Ingredients

- Large Portobello mushroom caps with gills removed
- Halved cherry tomatoes
- Shredded fresh mozzarella
- Fresh basil
- Olive oil

Instructions

- Get the oven preheated to 400 degrees get the baking sheet lined with foil the brush the caps and the rims of the mushrooms with oil.
- Slice the cherry or the grape tomatoes into half then place into a bowl as you drizzle with oil. Add chopped basil, pepper and salt the allow it to stay for some minutes as the flavors melt.

- Place cheese at the bottom of mushroom cap then add basil mixture, tomato and bakes for about8 minutes or until the cheese melts and the mushrooms well cooked.
- Remove from the oven then serve and enjoy.

Nutritional value

Calories	101
Fat	5g
Carbohydrate	12g
Fiber	1g
Protein	2g

4. Mediterranean grilled chicken

Preparation and cooking time – 22 minutes

Serves– 4

Ingredients

- Minced garlic cloves – 10
- Paprika – ½ teaspoon
- Ground nutmeg – ½ teaspoon
- Allspice – ½ teaspoon
- Ground green cardamom – ¼ teaspoon
- Olive oil – 6 tablespoons
- Skinless and boneless chicken thighs – 8
- Lemon juice – 2
- Sliced red onion – 1 medium

Instructions

- Mix together in a bowl minced garlic, olive oil and spices then pat the chicken thighs and rub each with the mixture.
- Place the chicken thighs into a large bowl on red onions then sprinkle olive oil two tablespoons and lemon juice on the chicken.
- Cover the bowl then refrigerate for about overnight.
- Heat the grill to medium then place the chicken over the grill cover and allow to cook for about 6 minutes.
- Turn the chicken over then grill for another 6 minutes
- Serve once ready and enjoy.

Nutritional value

Calories	172
Fat	12.8g
Carbohydrate	11.2g
Fiber	0g
Protein	6g

5. Mediterranean chicken tray bake

Preparation and cooking time – 45 minutes

Serves– 4

Ingredients

- Deseeded red peppers - 2
- Red onions – 1
- Chicken breasts - 4
- Full fat garlic and soft cheese herb – ½ x 150g
- Cherry tomatoes – 200g
- Black olives handful

Instructions

- Get the oven preheated to 350ºF then mix the onions and the peppers on a baking tray with part of the oil.
- Transfer to the oven then cook for about 10 minutes then create a pocket below the skin of each of chicken

breasts then place equal amounts of the cheese below the skin then smooth back the skin as you brush with the remaining oil.

- Season it then add to the tray with olives and tomatoes then return back to the oven as you cook for about 30 minutes or until the chicken turns golden and well cooked.
- Serve it with some baked potatoes and enjoy.

Nutritional value

Calories	401
Fat	21g
Carbohydrate	9g
Fiber	3g
Protein	45g

6. Silky smooth white bean hummus

Preparation and cooking time – 15 minutes

Serves– 6

Ingredients

- Chopped clove garlic
- White beans – 14 ½ ounces
- Tahini – ¼ cup
- Ranch dressing – 1/3 cup
- Black pepper – ¼ teaspoon
- Toasted pine nuts – 1 ½ tablespoons
- Kosher salt – ¼ teaspoon
- Fresh lemon juice – 3 tablespoons
- Water – ¼ cup

Instructions

- Place garlic, tahini, beans and olive oil into food processor then process for about 20 seconds. Scrape the sides the blend for another 20 seconds.
- Add bean water, black pepper, lemon juice and salt then puree for about two minutes or until smooth.
- Serve into a dish then garish and enjoy.

Nutritional value

Calories	250
Fat	2g
Carbohydrate	26g
Fiber	8g
Protein	9g

7. Simple fish stew

Preparation and cooking time – 25 minutes

Serves– 2

Ingredients

- Fennel seeds – 1 teaspoon
- Diced carrots – 2
- Olive oil – 1 tablespoon
- Finely chopped garlic cloves – 2
- Can chopped tomatoes – 400g
- Hot fish stock – 500ml
- Skinless Pollock fillets – 2
- Shelled king prawns – 85g

Instructions

- Place a large pan over medium heat then add the fennel seeds, celery, carrots, and garlic then cook for about 5 minutes.
- Add the leeks, stock and tomatoes then bring to boil and cover to simmer for about 20 minutes or until the vegetables become tender and the sauce thickened and reduced.
- Add fish, prawns then scatter and cook for about 2 minutes.
- Serve into bowls with a spoon

Nutritional value

Calories	346
Fat	8g
Carbohydrate	20g
Fiber	11g
Protein	42g

8. Creamy tomato risotto

Preparation and cooking time – 40 minutes

Serves– 4

Ingredients

- Can chopped tomato – 400g
- Vegetable stock – 1
- Knob of butter
- Olive oil – 1 tablespoon
- Finely chopped onion – 1
- Finely chopped garlic cloves – 2
- Finely chopped rosemary sprig – 1
- Cherry tomato – 300g
- Grated parmesan – 4 tablespoons
- Roughly torn basil – small
- Risotto rice – 250g

Instructions

- Place the chopped tomatoes and half of the stock into the food processor then pulse until smooth. Pour the mixture into the saucepan together with the remaining stock then bring to simmer and allow to stay over low heat.
- Place oil and butter into a sauce pan then heat until the butter gets melted. Add onions then cook for about 8 minutes then stir in rosemary and garlic and cook for 1 more minute. Add in the risotto rice and cook for a minute.
- As the risotto cooks, add hot stock and the tomato mixture then stir then add cherry tomatoes. Cook for about 25 minutes until the tomatoes soften.
- Cover and allow to stay for a minute then add basil.
- Serve in a dish then sprinkle with parmesan and ground black pepper.

Nutritional value

Calories	381
Fat	10g
Carbohydrate	61g
Fiber	4g
Protein	13g

9. Savory bean spinach soup

Preparation and cooking time – 2hr 40 minutes

Serves– 6

Ingredients

- Finely chopped onion – ½ cup
- Minced cloves garlic – 2
- Ground black pepper – ¼ teaspoon
- Coarsely chopped kale leaves or fresh spinach
- Finely shredded parmesan cheese

Instructions

- Combine tomato puree, rice, beans, onion broth, beans, basil, pepper, salt and garlic into the slow cooker.
- Cover then cook over high heat for about 2 ½ hours
- Add spinach into the soup then serve with cheese.

Nutritional value

Calories	148
Fat	1g
Carbohydrate	31g
Fiber	5g
Protein	8g

10.   Rosemary Chicken

Preparation and cooking time – 3hr 30 minutes

Serves– 1

Ingredients

- Frozen artichoke hearts – 1 (9 ounce)
- Boneless chicken breast halves – 1 ½ pounds
- Minced cloves garlic – 12
- Chopped onion – ½ cup
- Sodium chicken broth – ½ cup
- Finely grated lemon zest – 1 teaspoon
- Ground black pepper – ½ teaspoon
- Cornstarch – 1 tablespoon
- Cold water – 1 tablespoon
- Lemon wedges for garnishing – 2 lbs

Instructions

- Coat nonstick skillet with cooking spray then place over medium heat. Then add chicken and cook until browned. Combine the frozen artichoke hearts with onion into a small bowl then add rosemary, broth, pepper and lemon zest. Pour the mixture over vegetables into a slow cooker.
- Add browned chicken and garlic mixture over chicken. Cook for 3 ½ hours over high heat.
- Transfer artichokes and chicken to platter as you reserve the cooking liquid. Cover the chicken and the artichokes to keep it warm.
- Stir in the liquid into the slow cooker then cover and cook for about 15 minutes until it thickens. Add sauce over the chicken and the artichokes then serve with the lemon wedges.

Nutritional value

Calories	172
Fat	3g
Carbohydrate	8g
Fiber	2g
Protein	27g

11. Hassel back Caprese Chicken

Preparation and cooking time – 50 minutes

Serves– 3

Ingredients

- Boneless and skinless chicken breasts – 2 (8 ounces)
- Ground pepper – ½ teaspoon
- Sliced tomato – 1
- Prepared pesto – ¼ cup
- Broccoli florets – 8 cups
- Fresh mozzarella sliced and halved – 3 ounces
- Virgin florets – 8 cups
- Extra virgin olive oil

Instructions

- Get the oven preheated to 375°F then have the baking sheet coated with cooking spray.
- Cut the chicken breasts crosswise then sprinkle with salt and pepper. Fill the cuts with mozzarella and tomato slices then brush with pesto.
- Transfer the chicken to a side of the baking sheet.
- Add broccoli, oil, pepper and salt into a bowl with any remaining tomato slices then mix them in. Transfer the mixture of broccoli to the side of the baking sheet.
- Bake the chicken and the broccoli for about 25 minutes or until the broccoli gets tender and the chicken no longer pink.
- Remove from the oven then serve and enjoy.

Nutritional value

Calories	355
Fat	19g
Carbohydrate	10g
Fiber	4g
Protein	38g

12. Sausage, brussels sprout and potato soup

Preparation and cooking time – 45 minutes

Serves– 4

Ingredients

- Extra virgin olive oil – 3 tablespoons
- Italian sausage with casing removed – 8 ounces
- Diced onion – 1 cup
- Diced carrot – ½ cup
- Smoked paprika – 2 teaspoons
- Sliced baby yellow potatoes – 12 ounces
- Trimmed brussels sprouts – 8 ounces
- Chicken broth low sodium – 4 cups
- Red wine vinegar – 2 tablespoons
- Ground pepper – ½ teaspoon
- Chopped flat leaf parsley – ¼ cup

Instructions

- Place a cooking pan over medium heat then add sausage and cook as you stir occasionally for about 5 minutes. Add paprika, garlic then cook as you stir for about 30 seconds then add potatoes, broth, potatoes and brussels sprouts then bring to boil over medium heat.
- Reduce the heat for it to simmer and continue cooking as you stir until the potatoes becomes tender or for about 8 minutes.
- Add in the sausage, salt and pepper and vinegar then serve as you garnish with parsley.

Nutritional value

Calories	358
Fat	21g
Carbohydrate	31g
Fiber	5g
Protein	15g

13. Broccoli, chickpea and pomegranate salad

Preparation and cooking time – 20 minutes

Serves– 6

Ingredients

- Red onion thinly sliced – ¼ cup
- Ground cumin – ½ teaspoon
- Whole milk plain yoghurt – 1/3 cup
- Extra virgin olive oil – 2 tablespoons
- Tahini – 2 tablespoons
- Lemon juice – 1 tablespoon
- Ground pepper – ½ teaspoon
- Broccoli florets – 4 cups
- Low sodium chickpeas – 1 15 ounce
- Pomegranate seeds – ½ cup

Instructions

- Add cold water into a small bowl then soak the onions and allow to stay for about 10 minutes and drain well.
- Place a skillet over medium heat then add cumin and cook until fragrant. Transfer to a bowl then add yoghurt, lemon juice, oil, tahini, salt and pepper then whisk together until smooth.
- Add chickpeas, broccoli, pomegranate, seeds and onion then toss to combine and allow to stay for about 10 minutes.
- Season with salt then toss again then enjoy.

Nutritional value

Calories	162
Fat	9g
Carbohydrate	16g
Fiber	4g
Protein	6g

14. Lemon thyme roasted chicken with fingerlings

Preparation and cooking time – 20 minutes

Serves– 2

Ingredients

- Extra virgin olive oil or canola oil – 4 teaspoons
- Crushed dried thyme - ½ teaspoon
- Freshly ground black pepper – ½ teaspoon
- Fingerling potatoes – 1 pound
- Boneless chicken breast – 4 (1 ¼ pounds)
- Minced cloves garlic – 2
- Thinly sliced lemon – 1

Instructions

- Place a skillet over medium heat then add olive oil 2 teaspoons. Add thyme, pepper and salt into the skillet then stir. Add potatoes then toss to coat. Cover and allow to cook for about 12 minutes as you stir twice.

- Add the potatoes then push to the side of the skillet. Add the remaining oil then arrange the chicken halves on the side of the skillet then cook while uncovered for about 5 minutes.
- Turn the chicken then spread garlic over the chicken breast halves as you sprinkle the remaining with half teaspoon of thyme. Arrange the lemon slices over chicken then cover and allow to cook for about 7 minutes or until the potatoes are tender.
- Serve and enjoy

Nutritional value

Calories	255
Fat	6g
Carbohydrate	21g
Fiber	3g
Protein	29g

15. Garlic Hummus

Preparation and cooking time – 20 minutes

Serves– 8

Ingredients

- Chickpeas - 1 (15 ounce)
- Tahini – ¼ cup
- Extra virgin olive oil – ¼ cup
- Lemon juice – ¼ cup
- Ground cumin – 1 teaspoon
- Chili powder – ½ teaspoon
- Salt

Instructions

- Drain the chickpeas and reserve some liquid ¼ cup. Transfer the chickpeas to the food processor including the reserved liquid.

- Add tahini, garlic, lemon juice, oil, chili powder, cumin and salt. Puree until it becomes smooth for about 3 minutes.

Nutritional value

Calories	215
Fat	12g
Carbohydrate	10g
Fiber	2g
Protein	22g

16.Avocado Pesto

Preparation and cooking time – 20 minutes

Serves– 8

Ingredients

- Bunch of fresh basil – 1
- Ripe avocados – 2
- Hemp seeds or walnuts – ½ cup
- Lemon juice – 2 tablespoons
- Fine sea salt – ½ teaspoon
- Olive oil – ½ cup
- Ground pepper

Instructions

- Remove the basil leaves from their stems then add to the food processor with avocadoes, lemon juice, walnuts, garlic and salt then pulse until chopped finely. Add oil then process until a thick paste forms and season with pepper.

Nutritional value

Calories	126
Fat	13g
Carbohydrate	3g
Fiber	2g
Protein	1g

17. Fig and Ricotta Socca

Preparation and cooking time – 1 hr 15 minutes

Serves– 4

Ingredients

- In a large bowl add flour, salt and pepper then combine. Add water and whisk until smooth the allow it to rest for some time.
- Get the oven preheated to 450°F then place the cast iron skillet in the oven's lower rack.
- Get the hot pan from the oven then add a tablespoon of oil. Add batter into the pan then swirl so as to coat. Top

with the ricotta and figs then bake for about 20 minutes until the edges become crispy and the bottom browned.

- Use a pastry brush to remove from the oven. Get the broiler to high then broil the socca for about 3 minutes or until browned
- Drizzle with honey then cut into wedges and enjoy.

Nutritional value

Calories	239
Fat	11g
Carbohydrate	26g
Fiber	4g
Protein	9g

18.Plank Grilled Miso Salmon

Preparation and cooking time – 30 minutes

Serves– 4

Ingredients

- Maple syrup – 1 tablespoon
- Sake – 1 tablespoon
- White miso – ¼ cup
- Mayonnaise – ¼ cup
- Lemon zest – ½ teaspoon
- Skinned salmon fillet – 1 ½ pounds
- Scallions, trimmed
- Ground pepper – ¼ teaspoon
- White sesame seeds – 2 teaspoons

Instructions

- Place a saucepan over medium heat then add maple syrup and sake then cook. Remove from heat then add miso and cook until smooth. Allow it to cool for a minute then add lemon zest and mayonnaise.
- Set the grilling then place the plank with the smooth side facing downwards over the flame then grill until the bottom gets smoky and charred for about 4 minutes then set aside to cool.
- Remove the bones from the salmon using tweezers then place scallions on the side that's charred. Place salmon on scallions then season with pepper. Spread the glaze as you also sprinkle with the sesame seeds.
- Grill the fish over indirect heat and let it grill until the glaze starts bubbling and the fish well cooked for about 20 minutes.
- Serve on a plank or as desired.

Nutritional value

Calories	357
Fat	17g
Carbohydrate	10g
Fiber	1g
Protein	35g

19. Meditteranean Spiced Salmon and Vegetable Quinoa

Preparation and cooking time – 30 minutes

Serves– 4

Ingredients

Quinoa

- Uncooked quinoa – 1 cup
- Cucumbers seeded and diced – ¾ cup
- Koshcr salt – ½
- Sliced cherry tomatoes – 1 cup
- Finely diced red onion – ¼ cup
- Basil leaves – 4
- Lemon zest – 1

Salmon

- Black pepper - ¼ teaspoon
- Kosher salt – ½ teaspoon
- Cumin – 1 teaspoon

- Paprika – ½ teaspoon
- Salmon fillets – 20 ounces
- Fresh chopped parsley – ¼ cup
- Lemon wedges – 8

Instructions

- I a saucepan add quinoa with two cups of water and salt then bring to boil. Cover then cook allow to cook for about 20 minutes then put off the heat once ready and allow to rest for about 5 minutes. Mix the cucumbers, onions, tomatoes, basil, salmon and lemon zest.
- In a different bowl combine cumin, pepper, salt and paprika then line the baking pan with foil as you lightly grease with olive oil and non stick cooking spray.
- Transfer the salmon filets to the pan then coat evenly the fillets on the surface with about ½ teaspoon of spice mixture.
- Place lemon wedges by the edge of the pan together with salmon.
- Broil it in the oven for about 10 minutes or until the salmon gets cooked with flakes apart.
- Sprinkle it with parsley as you serve with the vegetable quinoa and roasted lemon wedges.

Nutritional value

Calories	222
Fat	4g
Carbohydrate	16g
Fiber	1g
Protein	32g

20. Mediterranean stuffed peppers

Preparation and cooking time – 1 hour

Serves– 4

Ingredients

- Olive oil or cooking oil of good quality
- Chopped yellow onion – 1
- Ground beef – ½ lb
- Garlic powder ½ teaspoon
- Canned or cooked chickpeas – 1 cup
- Ground beef – ½ lb
- Allspice – ½ teaspoon
- Salt and pepper
- Chopped parsley – ½ cup
- Short grain rice that's soaked in water for about 15 minutes then drained.
- Hot paprika – ½ teaspoon
- Bell peppers (tops removed) – 6 of any colors
- Chicken broth - ¾ cup

Instructions

- Place a heavy pot over heat then add oil 1 tablespoon and chopped onions then sauté until golden. Add meat then cook on medium heat as you stir occasionally until browned. Season the meat with salt, allspice, pepper and garlic powder. Stir in the chickpeas and allow to briefly cook.
- Add parsley to the same pot, paprika, rice and tomato sauce then stir to combine. Add water and allow to simmer until the liquid reduces.
- Reduce the heat to low then cover and cook for about 20 minutes or until rice is well cooked. As the rice cooks heat the grill to high the grill the bell peppers for about 15 minutes then remove and allow to cool.
- Get the oven preheated to 350ºF then place the bell peppers with the open side up into a baking dish that's filled with broth or water. Stuff the peppers with the rice mixture to the top the cover the dish and place into the oven.
- Bake for about 30 minutes then remove from the oven once ready.
- Garnish with parsley and serve immediately.

Nutritional value

Calories	250
Fat	6g
Carbohydrate	32g
Fiber	2g
Protein	24g

21. Herb crusted Mediterranean pork

Preparation and cooking time – 35 minutes

Serves– 4

Ingredients

- Pork tenderloin – 1 pound
- Dried oregano – 2 teaspoons
- Olive tapenade – 3 tablespoons
- Feta cheese – 1 ounce
- Lemon pepper – ¾ teaspoon

Instructions

- Place pork into a plastic wrap then rub the tenderloin with oil, lemon pepper, sprinkle oregano over the surface evenly then wrap tightly and refrigerate.
- Prepare a hot fire grill then unwrap the pork. Cut the tenderloin so that it lies flat then spread the olive tapenade on part of the tenderloin. Sprinkle it with cheese then fold back to the original shape.
- Grill the tenderloin over direct heat without covering for about 20 minutes. Turn it halfway in the grilling process then transfer the n transfer to the cutting board once ready. Allow to rest for about 10 minutes then remove and serve.

Nutritional value

Calories	540
Fat	11g
Carbohydrate	42g
Fiber	4g
Protein	34g

22. Mediterranean pork tenderloin with couscous

Preparation and cooking time – 1hr 30 minutes

Serves– 4

Ingredients

- Chicken broth – 1 cup
- Garlic cloves – 4
- Garam masala – 1 tablespoon
- Pork tenderloin – 2
- Cup couscous – 1 cu
- Raisins – ½ cup
- Olive oil – ½ cup
- Sliced almonds – ½ cup
- Fresh parsley – ½ cup
- Red wine vinegar – 2 tablespoons
- Salt and pepper

Instructions

- Combine broth with garlic 2 tablespoons into a slow cooker then mix together in a bowl garam masala, ground black pepper then pat the meat dry as you rub the mixture on the tenderloins.
- Place the tenderloins into a slow cooker then cover and cook for about 1 hour on normal heat. Transfer the tenderloins on a carving board and cover with foil. Pour the cooking drained from the pot into a cup then return one cup into the cooker.
- Add couscous and raisins into the liquid then cover and allow to cook for 15 minutes on high heat. Fluff the couscous using a fork then add almonds.
- To prepare parsley vinaigrette, add oil, vinegar and parsley with the remaining garlic into a bowl alongside pepper and salt to taste.
- Slice the tenderloins then transfer to the platter. Serve with parsley vinaigrette and couscous and enjoy.

Nutritional value

Calories	840
Fat	7g
Carbohydrate	51g
Fiber	6g
Protein	64g

23. Mediterranean Spaghetti

Preparation and cooking time – 40 minutes

Serves– 2

Ingredients

- Ounces Spaghetti – 6 ounces
- Olive oil – 1 tablespoon
- Clove garlic – 1 clove
- Sliced chorizo – 2 ounces
- Sundried tomato paste – ¼ cup
- Pitted black olives – ¼ cup
- Parsley leaves for garnishing

Instructions

- Get spaghetti cooked in a boiling salted water as per the given directions.
- Place a large skillet over medium over medium heat then add chorizo, garlic and then cook for about a

minute until crisp and golden. Add the tomato paste and the olives then cook for a minute.

- Drain the pasta then add sauce and season with ground black pepper and salt then toss to coat well.
- Serve then garnish with parsley.

Nutritional value

Calories	149
Fat	6g
Carbohydrate	21.3g
Fiber	3.6g
Protein	4g

24.   Mediterranean Naan Pizzas

Preparation and cooking time – 25 minutes

Serves– 2

Ingredients

- Garlic naan bread – 2
- Bulk Italian sausage – ½ lb
- Sundried tomatoes – 9
- Kalamata leaves – 6
- Peperoncini pepper – 1
- Cup pizza sauce – 1 cup
- Smoked havarti cheese shredded – 1 ½ cups

Instructions

- Get the oven preheated to 425°F
- Place the sausage into a skillet over medium heat then break into small bite pieces using your spatula then allow to simmer for about 10 minutes until done.

123

- Add the pizza sauce on the bread then lay the toppings as you also sprinkle with grated havarti.
- Allow to bake for about 10 minutes or until it browns with the cheese melted.
- Serve and enjoy

Nutritional value

Calories	500
Fat	34g
Carbohydrate	23g
Fiber	2g
Protein	24g

25. Italian sausage and vegetable stew

Preparation and cooking time – 25 minutes

Serves– 2

Ingredients

- Mild Italian sausages - 6 (cut into pieces)
- Diced tomato - 1 can
- Sliced zucchini – 2
- Minced cloves garlic – 4
- Can of tomato paste – 1 small

Instructions

- Place a skillet over medium heat then cook the sausages until browned.
- Combine the sausages, tomatoes, frozen vegetables, zucchini and garlic into a slow cooker then cook over medium heat for 2 hours or until the zucchini become tender.

Nutritional value

Calories	470
Fat	36g
Carbohydrate	18g
Fiber	5g
Protein	20g

Chapter 5

Snack Recipes

1. Mediterranean Hummus toast

Preparation and cooking time – 25 minutes

Serves– 2

Ingredients

- Seeded grain bread – 1
- TBS hummus – 2
- Ripe tomato – 2 slices
- Red onion – 2
- Roasted red pepper – 3 strips
- Crumbled feta cheese (Optional)
- Black olives

Instructions

- Spread the hummus on the toast bread slice then top with the tomato slices, cucumbers, red onion and the red pepper strips. Sprinkle with black olive slices and the feta cheese. Enjoy it as a snack.

Nutritional value

Calories	310
Fat	11g
Carbohydrate	42g
Fiber	8g
Protein	12g

2. Mediterranean New York style snack

Preparation and cooking time – 5 minutes

Serves– 2

Ingredients

- Hummus
- Sliced black olives
- Feta cheese crumbles
- Bagel crisps

Instructions

- Spread the humus over the bagel crisps then top with crumbled feta and black olives.

Nutritional value

Calories	150
Fat	5g
Carbohydrate	23g
Fiber	2g
Protein	7g

3. Chickpeas roasted with tamari and sea salt

Preparation and cooking time – 1 hr 15 minutes

Serves– 4

Ingredients

- Chickpeas – 1 can
- Olive oil – 1 tablespoon
- Tamari soy sauce – 3 tablespoons
- Sea salt – 1 teaspoon

Instructions

- Rinsed the canned beans using cold water then drain using a colander as you blot the remaining water using paper towels.
- Toss the beans with tamari, olive oil and allow to marinate for about 30 minutes.
- Get the oven preheated to350°F then arrange the chick peas in a nonstick baking sheet then bake as you stir

occasionally for about 60 minutes or until the chickpeas are crisp and dried.

- Serve warm or cold and enjoy.

Nutritional value

Calories	160
Fat	5g
Carbohydrate	26g
Fiber	4g
Protein	6g

4. Homemade savory rosemary sea salt crackers

Preparation and cooking time – 20 minutes

Serves– 4

Ingredients

- Flour – 2 cups
- Baking powder – 1 teaspoon
- Olive oil – 1/3 cup
- Salt – ½ teaspoon
- Rosemary for garnish

Instructions

- Mix flour, baking powder, water, olive oil and salt into a bowl then mix to create dough.
- Divide dough into half then roll out each on a cookie sheet
- Add the salt and rosemary or your preferred toppings then cut the dough using a sharp knife into squares.

- Get the even heated to 425ºF then bake the crackers until crispy and golden for about 14 minutes.
- Remove from the oven then serve and enjoy

Nutritional value

Calories	390
Fat	19g
Carbohydrate	49g
Fiber	3g
Protein	6g

5. Mediterranean Sandwich on Turkish Bread

Preparation and cooking time – 20 minutes

Serves– 2

Ingredients

- Prosciutto slices – 4
- Sliced roma potato – 1 ripe
- Baby spinach –
- Slices of hard cheese – 2
- Pesto – 2 tablespoons

Instructions

- Slice your preferred cobs bread into half then spread pesto on both the slices.
- Place prosciutto, spinach, tomato and cheese on the slices then top and enjoy.

Nutritional value

Calories	240
Fat	2g
Carbohydrate	53g
Fiber	0g
Protein	11g

6. Tortilla rollups

Preparation and cooking time – 25 minutes

Yields– 5

Ingredients

- Cream cheese – 8 ounces
- Sour cream – 8
- Whole grain onions – 5
- Chopped green chillies – 4 ounces
- Shredded cheddar cheese – ½ cup
- Green onions – 5
- Black olives – 2 tablespoons
- Flour tortillas – 12
- Picante sauce – 8 ounces

Instructions

- Combine cream cheese, green onions, sour cream cheddar cheese and chilies into the food processor then process until smooth.

- Roll tightly each tortilla then wrap in damp paper towels. Place into a tight plastic bag then refrigerate for some time until when ready to serve.
- Remove the tortillas from the paper towels and the bag then slice each crosswise then place a toothpick into each roll and serve with salsa for dipping or picante sauce.

Nutritional value

Calories	60
Fat	39g
Carbohydrate	6g
Fiber	0g
Protein	1g

7. Butter puff nachos

Preparation and cooking time – 15 minutes

Yields– 4

Ingredients

- Half roll packs of butter puff veggie - 2
- Salsa sauce – ¼ cup
- Cheese dip – ¼ cup
- Cheddar cheese – 2 slices
- Jalapeno or black olives for topping

Instructions

- Place butter puff veggie crackers in a serving dish until it covers the entire base then layer it cheddar cheese slices, cheese dip and salsa sauce.
- Microwave until the cheese melts then top with jalapenos and olives.

Nutritional value

Calories	150
Fat	12g
Carbohydrate	4g
Fiber	1g
Protein	6g

8. Mediterranean picnic snack

Preparation and cooking time – 10 minutes

Serves – 1

Ingredients

- Crusty whole wheat bread – 1 slice
- Cherry tomatoes – 10
- Oil cured olives – 6
- Olive oil

Instructions

Combine the bread pieces, cheese, olives and tomatoes in a serving platter then enjoy.

Nutritional value

Calories	197
Fat	9g
Carbohydrate	22g
Fiber	4g
Protein	7g

9. Eggcetera

Preparation and cooking time – 20 minutes

Serves – 2

Ingredients

- Hard boiled eggs (sliced) – 4
- Olive oil – 1 teaspoon
- Kosher salt – ½ teaspoon
- Paprika – ½ teaspoon

Instructions

- Dip the slices of eggs into oil then sprinkle with paprika and salt.

Nutritional value

Calories	88
Fat	6g
Carbohydrate	1g
Fiber	0g
Protein	6g

10.   Homemade granola

Preparation and cooking time – 40 minutes

Yields – 12

Ingredients

- Chopped dried mulberries – 1/3 cup
- Chopped dried strawberries – 1/3 cup
- Organic peanut butter – ½ cup
- Chopped raw cashews – ½ cup
- Mashed ripe bananas – 2 large
- Hemp protein powder – 2 tablespoons
- Raw sunflower seeds – 1/3 cup
- Rolled oats gluten free – 1 cup
- Flaxseed meal – 2 tablespoons
- Chia seeds – 2 tablespoons

Instructions

- Get the oven preheated to 350ºF then with parchment paper, line the baking pan then set aside.
- Combine peanut butter, mashed bananas in a bowl then use a hand held to whisk until smooth.
- Add the remaining ingredients into the bowl then use a spatula to mix until well combined. Transfer the mixture to the baking pan then press it down using a spatula until uniform on all sides.
- Bake for about 30 minutes. Allow the granola to cool for about 45 minutes while in the pan then cut into bars.
- Wrap the bars using a wax paper then put in an airtight container for about a week.

Nutritional value

Calories	209
Fat	11.8g
Carbohydrate	20.5g
Fiber	5.3g
Protein	8g

11. Statue Pita chips

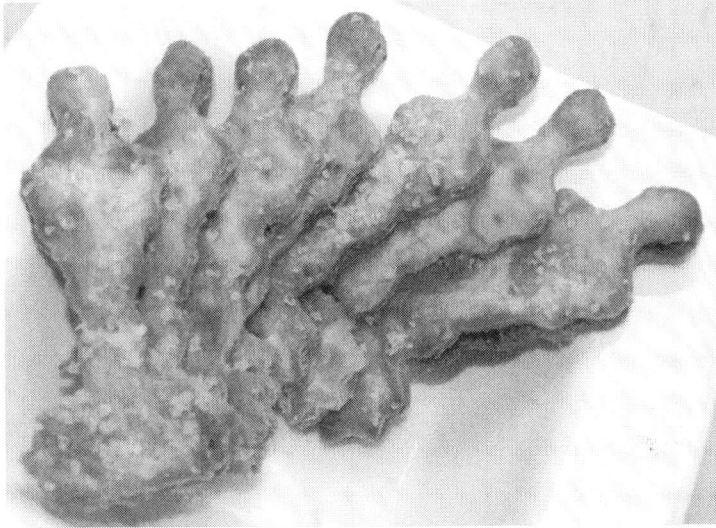

Preparation and cooking time – 20 minutes

Serves – 3

Ingredients

- Mediterranean pita breads – 6
- Olive oil
- Sea salt

Instructions

- Get the oven preheated to 350°F then line the baking sheet with foil
- Cut several statue pita breads then brush with olive oil but only on one side.
- Sprinkle with salt then bake for about 10 minutes. Rotate the tray then bake for 5 more minutes.
- Remove from the oven and allow to cool then serve with your preferred dip and enjoy.

Nutritional value

Calories	40
Fat	1g
Carbohydrate	7g
Fiber	1g
Protein	1g

12. Cheese granary bread

Preparation and cooking time – 1 hr 40 minutes

Serves – 4

Ingredients

- Granary bread flour (Dusting and kneading) – 3 cups
- Dry yeast (Active) – 2 teaspoon
- Olive oil – 2 tablespoon
- Grated mozzarella cheese - 1 cup
- Finely chopped jalapeno – ½ cup
- Black olives – ½ cup
- Sugar – 1 tablespoon
- Warm water – 1 ¼ cup

Instructions

- Warm water for proofing the yeast then add yeast and sugar and mix well.
- Set it aside for about 10 minutes for the yeast to frothy, bubbly and active.

- Mix flour and salt in another bowl then add the yeast mixture. Add oil and use a hand mixer to whisk it.
- Knead the flour once mixed until soft and sticky. Add flour if too welt or warm water if very dry.
- Leave it to rise in a place that's warm for about 1 hour as you grease the pan cake.
- Once ready place on a floored surface then use a rolling pin for rolling it into a rectangle shape.
- Spread the chopped jalapenos, cheese and olives on the surface leaving a small space on the sides.
- Roll the dough tightly into along log then place on a parchment then cut vertically as you keep one end intact.
- Braid together the pieces as you keep the part that's cut to the top then pinch the end.
- Lift the dough and place in the baking pan then join the ends. Add some cheese on top hen cover using a plastic wrap and allow to rise.
- To bake the bread, get the oven preheated to 380ºF then bake it for about 30 minutes or until it turns golden.
- Allow it to cool once ready for about 10 minutes then cut and serve as a snack.

Nutritional value

Calories	580
Fat	7g
Carbohydrate	79g
Fiber	4g
Protein	21g

13. Taco dip and chicken chips

Preparation and cooking time – 55 minutes

Serves – 3

Ingredients

- Sliced jicama – 1 large
- Sour cream – 1 (16oz)
- Softened cream cheese – 1 (8oz)
- Freshly shredded cheddar cheese – 1 cup
- Drained black olives – 1 can (optional)
- Shredded red leaf lettuce – ¼
- Chopped bell pepper
- Salsa/ chopped tomatoes

Instructions

- Mix in a large bowl, sour cream and cream cheese then mix and spread in a large serving dish. Top the mixture with bell pepper, cheese, lettuce, tomatoes/salsa and olives.

Nutritional value

Calories	220
Fat	18g
Carbohydrate	9g
Fiber	3g
Protein	7g

14. Pizza snack muffins

Preparation and cooking time – 50 minutes

Serves – 3

Ingredients

- Flour – 2 cups
- Basil – 1 teaspoon
- Oregano – 1 teaspoon
- Eggs – 1
- Non fat milk – ¾ cup
- Pepperoni – ½
- Black olives - 2 ¼ ounces
- Salad oil – 2 tablespoons
- Chopped tomatoes – ½ cup
- Shredded mozzarella cheese – ¾ cup

Instructions

- In a large bowl, add flour, basil, oregano and baking powder then add milk, oil and eggs. Stir until mixed then add pepperoni, tomatoes, half of the cheese and olives then mix well.
- Divide the batter equally into the oiled muffin cups then top with remaining cheese.
- Heat the oven to 350ºF until the muffins are browned or for about 35 minutes. Allow it to cool for 5 minutes then get off the pan.
- Serve warm or cool and enjoy.

Nutritional value

Calories	200
Fat	10g
Carbohydrate	21g
Fiber	1g
Protein	7g

15. Mediterranean hummus dip

Preparation and cooking time – 10

Serves - 4

Ingredients

- Hummus – 1 container
- Tomatoes
- Cucumber
- Feta cheese
- Mezzetta olives

Instructions

- Spread hummus into a serving dish then dice the olives, tomatoes and cucumbers then sprinkle hummus.
- Crumble feta cheese then sprinkle over the mixture
- Serve with pita chips, crackers of veggies.

Nutritional value

Calories	320
Fat	18g
Carbohydrate	30g
Fiber	4g
Protein	9g

Chapter 6

Dinner Recipes

1. Mediterranean Chicken Skillet

Preparation and cooking time – 25

Serves – 5

Ingredients

- Basil leaves – 1 teaspoon
- Oregano leaves – ½ teaspoon
- Garlic salt – 1 teaspoon
- Skinless and boneless chicken breasts – 1 ½ lb
- Rosemary leaves – ½ teaspoon
- Pepper – ¼ teaspoon

- Flour
- Oil – 2 tablespoons
- Onions – 1 large (cut into wedges)
- Green pepper – 1 large
- Diced tomatoes – 1 can
- Chicken broth – ½ can

Instructions

- In a bowl, mix six of the first ingredients the place aside. Coat the chicken using the spice mixture.
- Place a skillet over medium heat then add oil and chicken and allow to cook for about 3 minutes on each of the sides.
- Get chicken out of the skillet then add pepper and onion and cook for about 5 minutes. Add tomatoes, 2 tablespoons of flour mixture and broth then bring to boil as you stir frequently.
- Return the chicken back to the skillet as you reduce the heat. Cover and allow to simmer for about 10 minutes or until well cooked.

Nutritional value

Calories	220
Fat	15g
Carbohydrate	10g
Fiber	2g
Protein	3g

2. Mediterranean meatballs

Preparation and cooking time – 50

Yields – 10

Ingredients

- Ground beef – 2 lbs
- Chopped and sundried tomatoes – ¼ cup
- Chopped and roasted bell pepper – ¼ cup
- Chopped scallions – 2 tablespoons
- Chopped fresh parsley – 2 tablespoons
- Crumbled feta cheese – ¼ cup
- Garlic powder – ½ teaspoon
- Black pepper – ½ teaspoon
- Onion powder – ¼ teaspoon
- Chopped black olives – ¼ cup
- Salt

Instructions

- Get the oven preheated to 400°F then line then use foil to line the cookie sheet and grease the foil light.
- Combine all the ingredients in a bowl then form meat balls and place in the lined cookie sheet.
- Bake for about 15 minutes as you flip the meat balls and allow to cook for another 10 minutes.
- Remove from the oven then serve and enjoy.

Nutritional value

Calories	200
Fat	1g
Carbohydrate	1g
Fiber	0g
Protein	16g

3. Mediterranean Cubes

Preparation and cooking time – 35

Serves – 2

Ingredients

- Meat – 1 kilogram
- Lemon – 1
- Minced garlic – 1 teaspoon
- Ground black pepper – 1 teaspoon
- Chopped cilantro – 2 tablespoons
- Cumin – 1 teaspoon
- Salt – 1 pinch

Instructions

- Put all the ingredients into a bowl then cover with the lid. Let it marinate overnight. Squeeze the lemon and set aside.
- Place a pan over heat then once hot add meat then drizzle with oil then cook until the meat turns brown and tender.
- Serve it with the sliced tomato as you dress with extra virgin oil.

Nutritional value

Calories	290
Fat	10g
Carbohydrate	1g
Fiber	1g
Protein	17g

4. Mediterranean stuffed chicken breasts

Preparation and cooking time – 65

Serves – 4

Ingredients

- Red bell peppers – 1
- Pitted kalamata olives – 2 tablespoons
- Feta cheese crumbles – ¼ cup
- Boneless and skinless chicken breasts – 8
- Fresh basil

Instructions

- Preheat the boiler then cut the bell pepper into half as you discard the membranes and the seeds.
- Place the pepper halves with the skin sides up on a baking sheet as you flatten using your hands.
- Broil it for 15 minutes then place in a zipped plastic bag and allow to stay for about 15 minutes.

- Prepare the grill to medium heat then combine the bell pepper, cheese, basil and olives. Cut the thickest part of the chicken breast to form a pocket then add two tablespoons of the mixture into each.
- Close the opening then sprinkle the chicken breasts with black pepper and salt.
- Place on to the grill and grill for about 6 minutes.
- Remove from the grill hen cover with foil and allow to stay for about 10 minutes.

Nutritional value

Calories	210
Fat	6g
Carbohydrate	2g
Fiber	0.5g
Protein	35g

5. Garlic herb Mediterranean chicken with lem potatoes

Preparation and cooking time – 40 minutes

Serves – 4

Ingredients

- Gourmet garlic herb – 1 box kit (simply organic steam)
- Organic potatoes – 1.5 pounds
- Olive oil – 1 tablespoon
- Artichoke hearts – 1 (15 oz)
- Sundried tomatoes – ¼ cup
- Halved kalamata olives – ¼ cup
- Fresh lemon juice – 3 tablespoon
- Chicken breasts – 1 pound (cut in chunks)

Instructions

- Get the oven preheated to 400°F.
- In a bowl mix together potato cubes, lemon juice, herb seasoning and olive oil. Place the mixture into the parchment bag then fold twice as you lay on the baking sheet.
- Bake for about 35 minutes as the potatoes bake. Add together in a bowl artichoke hearts, chicken, sundried tomatoes, garlic herb seasoning and kalamata olives then mix together. Place the mixture in a parchment bag then fold and lay on a baking sheet near the potatoes.
- Bake for about 30 minutes then serve and enjoy.

Nutritional value

Calories	410
Fat	9g
Carbohydrate	50g
Fiber	16g
Protein	35g

6. Braised Mediterranean chicken with olives

Preparation and cooking time – 45 minutes

Serves – 4

Ingredients

- Chicken cut into pieces – 1 tablespoon
- Pitted kalamata olives – 1/3 cup
- Rosemary leaves – 2 teaspoons
- Orange juice   ½ cup
- Wine sauce – 1 jar
- Ground black pepper – ¼ teaspoon

Instructions

- Place a skillet over medium heat then add olive oil and heat. Add chicken then cook until browned then remove and set aside.
- Add rosemary, olives and garlic then cook over medium heat as you occasionally stir for about 2 minutes.
- Add orange juice, pepper and sauce then stir. Bring to boil as you cook over high heat then return the chicken in.
- Reduce the heat to low as you allow to simmer while covered for about 30 minutes or chicken is thoroughly cooked.
- Serve the chicken with sauce and cooked rice.

Nutritional value

Calories   730

Fat   6g

Carbohydrate   4g

Fiber   0g

Protein   127g

7. Mediterranean dip

Preparation and cooking time –

Serves – 6

Ingredients

- Crumbled feta cheese – 1 cup
- Small beefsteak tomatoes – 2
- Chopped scallions – 3
- Spiced sea salt – 1 teaspoon
- Olive oil – 1 ½ tablespoons

Instructions

- Sprinkle the cheese on a plate then top with chopped tomato as you also drizzle with olive oil.
- Sprinkle with scallions and spiced salt.
- Serve with either a spoon of tortilla or pita chips or as a topping on bread.

Nutritional value

Calories	35
Fat	25g
Carbohydrate	1g
Fiber	0g
Protein	2g

8. Mediterranean spiced beef and macaroni

Preparation and cooking time – 55

Serves – 4

Ingredients

- Ground beef – 1 lb
- Olive oil 2 tablespoons
- Minced cloves garlic – 3
- Diced onions – 1 cup
- Cayenne pepper – ¼ teaspoon
- Cinnamon – 1 teaspoon
- Ground cloves – ¼ teaspoon
- Red wine - ½ cup
- Parmesan cheese – ¼ cup
- Beef broth – 2 cups
- Tomato sauce – 8 ounces
- Roma tomatoes – 2
- Macaroni – 2 cups

Instructions

- Heat olive oil in a skillet then add onion, garlic and beef then cook. Drain grease from the cooked beef then add cinnamon, ground cloves, cayenne pepper and cook for about 4 minutes.
- Add tomatoes, red wine and tomato sauce then allow to simmer for about 5 minutes then add the noodles and stir together.
- Reduce the heat then cook for about 25 minutes or until the noodles become tender and the liquid cooled down.
- Top with grated parmesan cheese then serve and enjoy.

Nutritional value

Calories	630
Fat	28g
Carbohydrate	55g
Fiber	5g
Protein	34g

9. Mediterranean burger

Preparation and cooking time – 25

Serves – 4

Ingredients

- Lean ground beef – 1pound
- Artichoke hearts marinated with olive oil – 1/3 cup
- Grated asiago cheese – 1/3 cup
- Sun dried tomatoes marinated with olive oil – ¼ cup
- Minced garlic – 1 teaspoon
- Olive oil – 1 tablespoon
- Minced garlic – 1 teaspoon
- Olive oil - 1 tablespoon
- Fresh rosemary, thyme and oregano – 1 tablespoon
- Freshly ground black pepper
- Sea salt

Instructions

- Combine all the ingredients in a mixing bowl
- Heat oil in a pan then sauté then add the ground beef and cook for about a minute. Add the seasonings then cook as you adjust the taste accordingly.
- Shape the burgers as you heat the grill or preheat BBQ. Drizzle some of the olive oil of both sides of the burger. Place the burgers on the grill once ready then grill for about 4 minutes or until ready.
- Serve and enjoy.

Nutritional value

Calories	240
Fat	12g
Carbohydrate	6g
Fiber	1g
Protein	27g

10. Moroccan Beef Tajine

Preparation and cooking time – 1 hr 57mins

Serves – 4

Ingredients

- Stewing beef 800g
- Stewing beef
- Garlic cloves – 6
- Large onion – 1
- Butternut squash – 1
- Tinned tomatoes – 1 can
- Chickpeas – 1 can
- Prunes – 100g
- Vegetable stock – 1 litre
- Moroccan spice – 3 tablespoons
- Olive oil – 1 tablespoon
- Cinnamon – 1 tablespoon
- Cumin – 1 tablespoon

- Paprika – 1 tablespoon
- Coriander – 1 tablespoon
- Ground ginger – 1 tablespoon
- Red chili pepper
- Black olives salt and pepper

Instructions

- In a small bowl add seasonings mix well then chop the beef into small sizes. Rub seasonings then place in the fridge to stay for an hour.
- Peel garlic and onions then finely cut and place in the tajine. Add olive oil then cook for about 2 minutes over medium heat or until the onions gets soft. Add the beef and cook for 5 minutes.
- Mix together in a blender the tinned tomatoes, prunes, vegetable stock, drained chickpeas and tomato puree then add to the tajine. Let it boil then reduce the heat and allow to simmer for about 15 minutes.
- Deseed, peel and chop the butternut squash then add to into tajine and stir. Cover the lid and cook for 90 more minutes over medium heat.
- Add red chili peppers and the black olives then stir.
- Serve and enjoy with warm crusty bread.

Nutritional value

Calories   380

Fat   1g

Carbohydrate   74g

Fiber   13g

Protein   11g

11. Mediterranean shrimp bake

Preparation and cooking time – 1 hr 10 minutes

Serves – 4

Ingredients

- Olive oil – 3 tablespoons
- Garlic cloves – 2
- Pepper – ¾ teaspoon
- Coarse salt – ¾ teaspoon
- Large shrimp – 2 pounds (Peeled and deveined)
- Chopped parsley – ½ cup
- Crumbled feta cheese – 1 cup
- Lemon juice – 2 tablespoons

Instructions

- Peel, devein and clean the shrimp then keep it chilled until when ready to use.
- Get the oven preheated to 450ºF then mix together garlic, olive oil, parsley, lemon juice, pepper and feta.
- Pour tomato layer into a baking dish then top with raw shrimp. Cover the shrimp with tomato mixture that's remaining then bake for about 35 minutes or until he shrimp is ready.
- Stir in the remaining ingredients then bake for another 15 minutes.
- Serve and enjoy.

Nutritional value

Calories	210
Fat	18g
Carbohydrate	7g
Fiber	1g
Protein	7g

12. Cod with tomatoes and Kalamata Olives

Preparation and cooking time – 35

Serves – 2

Ingredients

- Olive oil – 1 tablespoon
- Dried oregano – 1 teaspoon
- Crushed red pepper ½ teaspoon
- Minced garlic cloves – 4
- Crushed fennel seeds – ½ teaspoon
- Crushed red pepper – ½ teaspoon
- Dry white wine – ½ cup
- Chopped kalamata olives – ½ cup
- Fresh cod filets – 1 ½ lbs

Instructions

- Place skillet over medium heat then add olive oil and garlic ten sauté for about 30 seconds or until fragrant.
- Add oregano, crushed red pepper, and fennel then cook for one more minute.
- Add the white wine as you increase the heat to high then simmer for about 3 minutes. Add tomatoes and the olives then simmer for about 5 minutes.
- Place cod fillets into the skillet then scoop some soup and pour over the top.
- Cover and allow to simmer for about 5 minutes or until the fish is tender and can flake easily with a fork.
- Serve the cod filets as you top with sauce.

Nutritional value

Calories	230
Fat	6g
Carbohydrate	10g
Fiber	3g
Protein	29g

13. Grilled lobster tails

Preparation and cooking – 22 minutes

Serves – 3

Ingredients

- Lobster tails – 6
- Olive oil – ¼ cup
- Fresh lemon juice – ¼ cup
- Fresh dill – 1 tablespoon
- Salt – 1 teaspoon

Instructions

- Get the grill preheated to medium heat then cut the lobster tails lengthwise so as to expose the flesh.
- Pat with paper towels to dry then combine the ingredients in a bowl and mix until the salt dissolves. Brush that mixture onto the lobster tails then place onto the grill as you allow to cook for about 7 minutes.

- Turn the lobster during the cooking process and they should be done when the internal meat temperature reaches 140°F.
- Remove from the heat then serve

Nutritional value

Calories	290
Fat	14g
Carbohydrate	3g
Fiber	0g
Protein	38g

14. Roasted Ling Cod

Preparation and cooking time – 15

Serves – 2

Ingredients

Ling cod – 1 lb

Olive oil – 1 teaspoon

Black pepper

Salt

For olive tapenade

- Pitted kalamata olives – 12
- Sundried tomatoes – 2 tablespoons
- Basil leaves – 3
- Cloves garlic – 2
- Drained capers juice – 1 tablespoon
- Olive oil – 3 table spoons

Instructions

- Get the oven preheated to 400 degrees then sprinkle the fish with salt and pepper as you drizzle with olive oil.
- Create a parchment paper for enclosing the fish then place on a baking dish and let it bake for about 15 minutes or until the fish is well cooked.
- Combine sundried tomatoes, basil leaves, olives, garlic cloves into a food processor then pulse until well chopped. Drizzle with olive oil and pulse again to combine.
- Transfer tapenade into a bowl then stir in capers as you add the lemon juice to taste then set aside.
- Spoon tapenades over the fish then serve immediately.

Nutritional value

Calories	550
Fat	33g
Carbohydrate	23g
Fiber	2g
Protein	43g

15. Honey garlic salmon

Preparation and cooking time – 20

Serves – 4

Ingredients

- Butter – ¼ cup
- Honey – ¼ cup
- Freshly squeezed lemon – 2
- Salmon fillets (wild caught) – 4
- Lemon wedges
- Salt to taste

Instructions

- Get the oven preheated to broil then in a skillet, add butter then cook until golden brown then add honey, garlic, and sauté for about 1 minute until fragrant. Add lemon juice then stir well and combine the flavors.

- Add salmon steaks to the skillet then cook each piece for about 4 minutes or until golden then season with pepper and salt to taste.
- Add lemon wedges around the salmon then transfer to the oven. Grill for about 6 minutes or until nicely charred.
- Drizzle with brown butter sauce then serve with some steamed vegetables over salad or rice.

Nutritional value

Calories	410
Fat	26g
Carbohydrate	21g
Fiber	1g
Protein	23g

16. Garlic Chicken

Preparation and cooking time – 40 minutes

Serves – 6

Ingredients

- Chicken thighs – 6
- Butter o 6 tablespoons
- Honey – ¼ cup
- Minced garlic – 1 tablespoon
- Lemon juice freshly squeezed – 2
- Chicken broth – 4 tablespoons
- Broccoli florets – 3 cups
- Salt and pepper to taste

Instructions

- Preheat the oven to broil over medium heat then pat the chicken with paper towel to dry as you season with pepper and salt. Melt butter 1 tablespoon in a skillet

185

then sear the chicken thighs until the skin gets crispy for about 5 minutes.

- Drain excess oil from the pan and leave about 2 tablespoons for added flavor then transfer chicken to a plate and set aside.

For the sauce

- Melt butter using the same skillet then add butter and cook for about 3 minutes then add honey and garlic then sauté for about 1 minute or until fragrant. Add lemon juice then stir so as to combine all the flavors.
- Add chicken back to the pan then cook for about 5 minutes with the sauce. Reduce the heat then cover the skillet and cook until done. Add salt and pepper to season and about 3 spoons of chicken broth.
- Transfer the skillet to the oven then grill for 3 more minutes. Serve the chicken with lemon wedges as you garnish with parsley and drizzle with juices from the pan.
- You can serve with rice, noodles or steamed vegetables.

Nutritional value

Calories	198
Fat	2g
Carbohydrate	18.3g
Fiber	0g
Protein	27.5g

17. Mediterranean Edamame Toss

Preparation and cooking time – 55

Serves – 4

Ingredients

- Uncooked quinoa – ½ cup (rinsed and drained)
- Sweet soya beans (Edamame) – 1 cup
- Fresh spinach or aragula leaves – 1 cup
- Chopped red onion – ½ cup
- Olive oil – 2 tablespoons
- Lemon juice – 2 tablespoons
- Crumbled feta cheese – ¼ cup
- Snipped fresh basil – 2 tablespoons
- Freshly ground pepper – ¼ teaspoon
- Water – 1 cup
- Salt – ¼ teaspoon

Instructions

- In a saucepan add quinoa and water then place over heat and cook to boil. Cover and allow to simmer for about 15 minutes or until the quinoa is tender then add edamame and cook for 4 minutes.
- In a large bowl, mix quinoa, aragula, tomato and onion and in another bowl add olive oil, olive peel and lemon juice then mix. Add basil, cheese, salt and pepper. Add quinoa mixture then toss to coat.
- Sprinkle the remaining cheese then serve while at room temperature and enjoy.

Nutritional value

Calories	236
Fat	12g
Carbohydrate	23g
Fiber	5g
Protein	11g

18. Spiralized Mediterranean cucumber salad

Preparation and cooking time – 40

Serves – 6

Ingredients

- Red wine vinegar – 2 tablespoons
- Olive oil – ½ cup
- Freshly chopped oregano – 1 tablespoon
- Salt and pepper – ¼
- Cucumber – 1 large
- Halved cherry tomatoes – 1 cup
- Thinly sliced red onion – ½ cup
- Cubed feta cheese – ½ cup
- Pitted kalamata olives – ¼ cup

Instructions

- In a large bowl add oregano, vinegar, salt and pepper then add the spiralized cucumbers, onion, tomatoes and olives. Toss the mixture to toss with dressing then serve as you top with more oregano as desired.

Nutritional value

Calories   149

Fat   13g

Carbohydrate   5g

Fiber   1g

Protein   14g

19. Sicilian Pepper Salad

Preparation and cooking time – 1 hr

Serves – 6

Ingredients

- Olive oil – 3 tablespoons
- Red bell peppers – 3
- Italian frying peppers – 5
- Cloves garlic sliced – 4
- Dry white wine – 1 tablespoon
- White wine vinegar – 1/3 cup
- Sugar – 1 tablespoon
- Kosher salt -3/4 teaspoon
- Currants – ½ cup
- Toasted pine nuts – 1/3 cup
- Chopped fresh parsley – 2 tablespoons

Instructions

- Place a large skillet over medium heat then add peppers and cook for about 5 minutes. Add wine and garlic then cook until tender or for about 3 minutes. Add sugar, vinegar and salt then cook for a minute. Remove the mixture from the heat then add the currants and stir add pine nuts.
- Sprinkle with parsley as you serve.

Calories	142
Fat	9g
Carbohydrate	14g
Fiber	3g
Protein	2g

20. Grilled shrimp skewers with white bean salad

Preparation and cooking time – 1 hr

Serves - 6

Ingredients

- Lemon zest finely grated- 1 teaspoon
- Lemon juice – 1/3 cup
- Olive oil – 3 tablespoons
- Minced fresh oregano – 2 tablespoons
- Minced fresh chives – 2 tablespoons
- Freshly ground pepper – 1 teaspoon
- Rinsed cannellini – 2 cans
- Cherry tomatoes – 12
- Finely diced celery – 1 cup
- Raw shrimp – 24

Preparation

- Combine in a large bowl, lemon zest oregano, oil, lemon juice, chives, sage, pepper and salt. Add tomatoes, beans and celery into the bowl then toss to combine.
- Get the grill preheated to medium heat then thread shrimp onto the skewers.
- Grill the shrimp until firm and pink as you turn once for about 4 minutes. Serve the shrimp with white bean salad then drizzle with dressing.

Calories	212
Fat	8g
Carbohydrate	22g
Fiber	8g
Protein	17g

Chapter 7

Dessert Recipes

1. Blueberries with lemon cream

Preparation and cooking time – 10 minutes

Serves – 4

Ingredients

- Break cream cheese using fork into a bowl then drain any liquid from the yoghurt.
- Add honey and yoghurt into the bowl then mix until creamy using an electric mixer then add lemon zest.

195

- Layer the blueberries and lemon cream in the dessert dishes.
- Serve immediately and enjoy.

Nutritional value

Calories	144
Fat	5g
Carbohydrate	21g
Fiber	2g
Protein	5g

2. Tomato basil skewers

Preparation and cooking time – 10 minutes

Serves – 6

Ingredients

- Fresh mozzarella balls – 16 small
- Fresh basil leaves – 16
- Cherry tomatoes – 16
- Olive oil
- Freshly ground pepper and coarse salt

Instructions

- Thread mozzarella, tomatoes and basil on small skewers then drizzle with oil
- Sprinkle with pepper and salt

Nutritional value

Calories	46
Fat	3g
Carbohydrate	1g
Fiber	0g
Protein	3g

3. Cherries with ricotta and toasted almonds

Preparation and cooking time – 10 minutes

Serves – 1

Ingredients

- Frozen pitted cherries – ¾ cup
- Part skim ricotta – 2 tablespoons
- Toasted slivered almonds – 2 tablespoons

Instructions

Microwave the cherries until warm for about 2 minutes then top almonds and ricotta.

Nutritional value

Calories	155
Fat	6g
Carbohydrate	22g
Fiber	3g
Protein	6g

4. Mediterranean summer sampler

Preparation and cooking time – 15

Serves – 2

Ingredients

- Raw almond – ¼ cup
- Sliced strawberries – 2
- Sliced figs – 2
- Feta – 6 cubes
- Sliced meat -3

Instructions

- Place everything on a serving platter then serve and enjoy.

5. Greek yoghurt dip

Preparation and cooking time – 20

Serves – 2

Ingredients

- Plain yoghurt – 1 cup
- Fresh mint leaves finely chopped – 1
- Kosher salt – ¼ tablespoons
- Fresh dill weed – 1 tablespoon
- Red wine vinegar – 1 tablespoon
- Olive oil – 1 tablespoon
- Pomegranate seeds – 1 tablespoon
- Green onion – 1

Instructions

In a small bowl add yoghurt, vinegar, mint, dill, salt and oil then combine well.

Garnish with onion slices and pomegranate seeds.

Nutritional value

Calories	100
Fat	0g
Carbohydrate	6g
Fiber	0g
Protein	17.3g

6. Honey pistachio roasted pears

Preparation and cooking time – 20 minutes

Serves – 6

Ingredients

- Barlett or bosc pears (peeled, cored and halved)
- Pear nectar ¼ cup
- Honey – 3 tablespoons
- Butter – 2 tablespoons
- Orange zest – 1 teaspoon
- Powdered sugar – 2 tablespoons
- Chopped, roasted and salted pistachios
- Mascarpone cheese – ½ cup

Instructions

Get the oven preheated to about 400°F. Arrange the pears in a baking dish then add the next four ingredients. Roast while uncovered for about 25 minutes as you occasionally spoon the liquid over the pears.

Transfer the pears to a serving dish then stir together powdered sugar and cheese. Spoon it over pears as you add pistachios. Drizzle with some more honey.

Nutritional value

Calories	250
Fat	15g
Carbohydrate	27g
Fiber	3g
Protein	3g

7. Strawberry Greek frozen yoghurt

Preparation and cooking time – 2 hr 25 minutes

Serves – 2

Ingredients

- Greek low fat yoghurt – 3 cups
- Lemon juice – ¼ cup
- Vanilla – 2 tablespoons
- Sliced strawberries

Instructions

- In a bowl, combine yoghurt, lemon juice, sugar, vanilla and salt then whisk together until smooth.
- Freeze the mixture into an ice cream maker as per the instructions then add sliced strawberries.

- Transfer to a container that's airtight then freeze for about 2 hours
- Remove from the freezer then allow it to stay for about 15 minutes before serving.

Nutritional value

Calories	86
Fat	1g
Carbohydrate	16g
Fiber	0g
Protein	4g

8. Mint Greek frozen yoghurt

Preparation and cooking time – 2 hr - 15

Serves - 2

Ingredients

- Greek low fat yoghurt – 3 cups
- Lemon juice – ¼ cup
- Sugar – 1 cup
- Vanilla – 2 teaspoons
- Snipped fresh mint – 2 tablespoons

Instructions

- In a bowl combine lemon juice, yoghurt, sugar, vanilla and salt then whisk until smooth.
- Freeze the mixture in an ice cream maker as per the instructions then add the mint. Transfer to a container that's airtight and let it freeze for about 2 hours.

- Remove from the freezer and allow to stay for about 15 minutes before serving.

Nutritional value

Calories	84
Fat	1g
Carbohydrate	15g
Fiber	0g
Protein	4g

9. Chocolate avocado mousse

Preparation and cooking time – 30

Serves – 4

Ingredients

- Avocadoes – 2
- Unsweetened cocoa powder – 1/3 cup
- Almond milk – ¼ cup
- Raw honey – 3 tablespoons
- Vanilla extract – ½ teaspoon
- Coconut whipped cream for garnish – 6 tablespoons
- Shaved dark chocolate – 1 ½ tablespoon

Instructions

- Halve and pit avocadoes then go ahead and scoop the flesh and place in the blender.
- Add the four ingredients that follow until well blended into a smooth and creamy mixture.

- Serve into bowls then top with chocolate shavings and whipped cream.

Nutritional value

Calories	19
Fat	5g
Carbohydrate	33g
Fiber	10g
Protein	5g

10.   Ricotta with orange blossom cherry

Preparation and cooking – 1 hr 30 minutes

Serves – 4

Ingredients

- Unsalted butter (for greasing)
- Milk ricotta cheese -1 ½ cups
- Honey – 3 tablespoons
- Lemon zest – 1 teaspoon
- Egg – 1

For cherry orange blossom

- Frozen cherries – 1 cup
- Sugar – 3 tablespoons
- Freshly squeezed orange – 2 tablespoons
- Orange blossom water – 1 teaspoon

Instructions

- To make ricotta custards: Get the oven heated to about 400ºF. Grease the ramekins with butter then place on the baking sheet. Add ricotta, zest, honey and egg into a bowl then mix until smooth.
- Divide the mixture into ramekins as you smooth the tops. Bake for about 35 minutes or until golden. Remove from the oven then allow to cool.
- To make cherry compote: place a saucepan over medium heat then add cherries, orange juice and sugar then cook as you occasionally stir for about 25 minutes. Remove from heat then add orange blossom water and allow it to slightly cool.
- Transfer the ramekins to the serving plates then spoon the syrup and the cherries over the top.

Nutritional value

Calories	125
Fat	4g
Carbohydrate	41g
Fiber	4g
Protein	14g

11. Fresh cherry sauce

Preparation and cooking time – 20 minutes

Yields – 3 cups

Ingredients

- Stemmed and pitted cherries – 1 ½ pounds
- Butter – 4 tablespoons
- Granulated sugar – ½ cup
- Water – ½ cup
- Cornstarch – 1 tablespoon

Instructions

- In a saucepan combine the ingredients then place over medium heat and bring to boil while stirring occasionally.

- Let it boil for three minutes then reduce and allow to simmer for 2 minutes. Get the cherry mixture off the heat then let it cool before services.
- Use an airtight container to store the leftovers then refrigerate.
- Warm the sauce before serving.

Nutritional value

Calories   87

Fat   3g

Carbohydrate   22g

Fiber   3g

Protein   1g

12. Mediterranean yoghurt cream

Preparation and cooking time – 15 minutes

Serves - 3

- Strawberries or raspberries – 250g
- Sugar – 4 tablespoon
- Vinsanto santorini wine – 50 ml
- Fresh cream – 284 ml
- Greek yoghurt – 284ml
- Sprigs fresh mint

Instructions

- Place the raspberries, into a bowl then add wine and sugar then set aside.

- Whip the cream in a separate bowl then add in the yoghurt. Mix half of the cream with yoghurt into raspberry mixture.
- Combine the remaining cream with the yoghurt mix for a ripple effect then divide into glasses.
- Top with a mint sprig and enjoy.

Nutritional value

Calories	61
Fat	3.3g
Carbohydrate	4.7g
Fiber	0g
Protein	3.5g

13. Almonds and Honey

Preparation and cooking time – 20

Serves – 2

Ingredients

- Water enough to cover the almonds
- Almonds – ¼ cup
- Hone – 4 tablespoons

Instructions

- Blanch the almonds by removing the skin then place in a cooking pot then add water and bring to boil.
- Add the almonds and allow to boil for about 60 seconds.
- Remove from water using a strainer then rinse with cold water.
- Remove almonds skin then dry using a paper towel. Add the almonds to a saucepan with honey 2 tablespoons

then place over medium heat. Cook the almonds until golden then remove from heat.

- Pour the almonds into small bowls then top with the remaining honey.
- Let the almonds cool then enjoy.

Nutritional value

Calories	162
Fat	13.7g
Carbohydrate	7.2g
Fiber	2.6g
Protein	5.3g

14. Greek yoghurt with berries and seeds

Preparation and cooking time – 10

Serves – 2

Ingredients

- Raspberries – handful
- Blueberries – handful
- Greek yoghurts – heaped tablespoon
- Sunflower seeds – 1 teaspoon
- Flaked almonds – 1 teaspoon
- Pumpkin seeds – 1 teaspoon

Instructions

- Wash all the berries then dry them up and place in a dish. Add Greek yoghurt alongside nuts and seeds then enjoy

Conclusion

Congratulations and thank you for taking your time to download Mediterranean Diet Cookbook. The information shared in this book if well implemented has the potential of enabling you to adopt the Mediterranean lifestyle successfully. Understanding the diet and knowing how to balance the foods effectively is key to realizing success with Mediterranean diet.

Now that you've read the book all through, you can go ahead and put whatever you've read into practice. Try out the recipes as you balance the meals in order to find out what works well for you. It's by trying that you'll get to know how to balance your meals in a way that leads to success with the diet.

I know that you've found the book to be valuable; would you please go ahead and leave a review for the book.

Thank you and enjoy Mediterranean Diet Lifestyle.

Printed in Great Britain
by Amazon